Living Through History

THE NAPOLEONIC WARS

GRAHAM MITCHELL

B.T. Batsford Ltd London

Contents

BRITAIN AND FRANCE AT WAR	3
MANNERS, MORALS AND MONARCHY	10
George Augustus Frederick, Prince of Wales	13
Beau Brummell	17
Jane Austen	21
RADICALISM AND REFORM	26
William Cobbett	28
Francis Place	32
William Blake	35
SOLDIERS AND SAILORS	39
Captain John Kincaid	43
John Shipp	48
Sir Sidney Smith	52
William Richardson	57
BOOKS FOR FURTHER READING	61
DATE LIST	62
INDEX	64

© Graham Mitchell 1989
First published 1989

All rights reserved. No part of this publication may be reproduced, in any form or by any means, without permission from the Publisher

Typeset by Tek-Art Ltd, West Wickham, Kent
Printed in Great Britain by
Courier International Ltd, Tiptree, Essex
for the publishers
B.T. Batsford Ltd
4 Fitzhardinge Street
London W1H 0AH

ISBN 0 7134 5729 5

HEATHFIELD SCHOOL
LIBRARY
Acc. No: 8018
30003709

Acknowledgments
The Author and Publishers would like to thank the following for their kind permission to reproduce copyright illustrations: British Library for figures 21, 32 and 44; reproduced by courtesy of the Trustees of the British Museum, figures 3, 4 and 22; Department of the Environment for figure 37; Hulton Picture Library for figures 6 and 9; Mansell Collection for figures 1, 5, 7, 8, 10, 11, 14, 16, 17, 18, 20, 23, 24, 25, 26, 27, 29, 31, 35, 36, 38, 40, 41, 42, 46, 48 and 49; Mary Evans Picture Library for figures 13 and 15; National Army Museum for figures 33, 34, 39 and 43; National Maritime Museum for figure 50; National Portrait Gallery for figures 19, 28, 30 and 45; Royal pavilion, Brighton for figure 12; Victoria and Albert Museum for figure 47.

Cover illustrations
The colour illustration on the front cover is a reproduction of *Scotland For Ever!*, 1881, by Lady Butler (Leeds City Art Galleries); the black and white illustrations are The Prince of Wales in Garter Robes, 1799 (Royal Pavilion, Brighton) and the Chimney Sweep's Boy (The Mansell Collection).

Frontispiece
Recruiting Party for the 33rd Regiment, 1813 by R. and D. Havell (The Mansell Collection)

The pictures were researched by Eva June Smith.

Britain And France At War

For a period of 22 years, from 1793 to 1815 Britain waged war with first Revolutionary, then Napoleonic, France. There were two brief respites, in 1802-3 and 1814. What began as a war to check France's avowed intention of carrying her revolutionary aims beyond her frontiers, had become, by 1800, a war to check the grandiose ambitions of her self-crowned Emperor, Napoleon I.

Napoleon Bonaparte, or "Boney" as the British quickly nicknamed him, not only changed the map of Europe during the years of his ascendancy, he also challenged all the great orthodoxies and established ideas and attitudes of his time. He sought to humble the crowned heads of Europe and to become its sole master; but for British sea-power, the grit and determination of Wellington's Penninsular army, and Napoleon's own folly in marching into the great wilderness of Russia in 1812, he would undoubtedly have succeeded.

A general at the age of 26, an Emperor at 30, Napoleon was a strategist of genius, shrewd in politics and bold in military situations, who achieved his success by consistently defeating his enemies on the battlefield. By 1802 only Britain thwarted his schemes for European domination. So, in that year he signed a treaty with the British government (The Peace of

1 Napoleon's preferred image of himself as the noble, heroic victor. This painting by Philippoteaux shows him surveying the scene of his famous victory at the Battle of Rivoli in 1797.

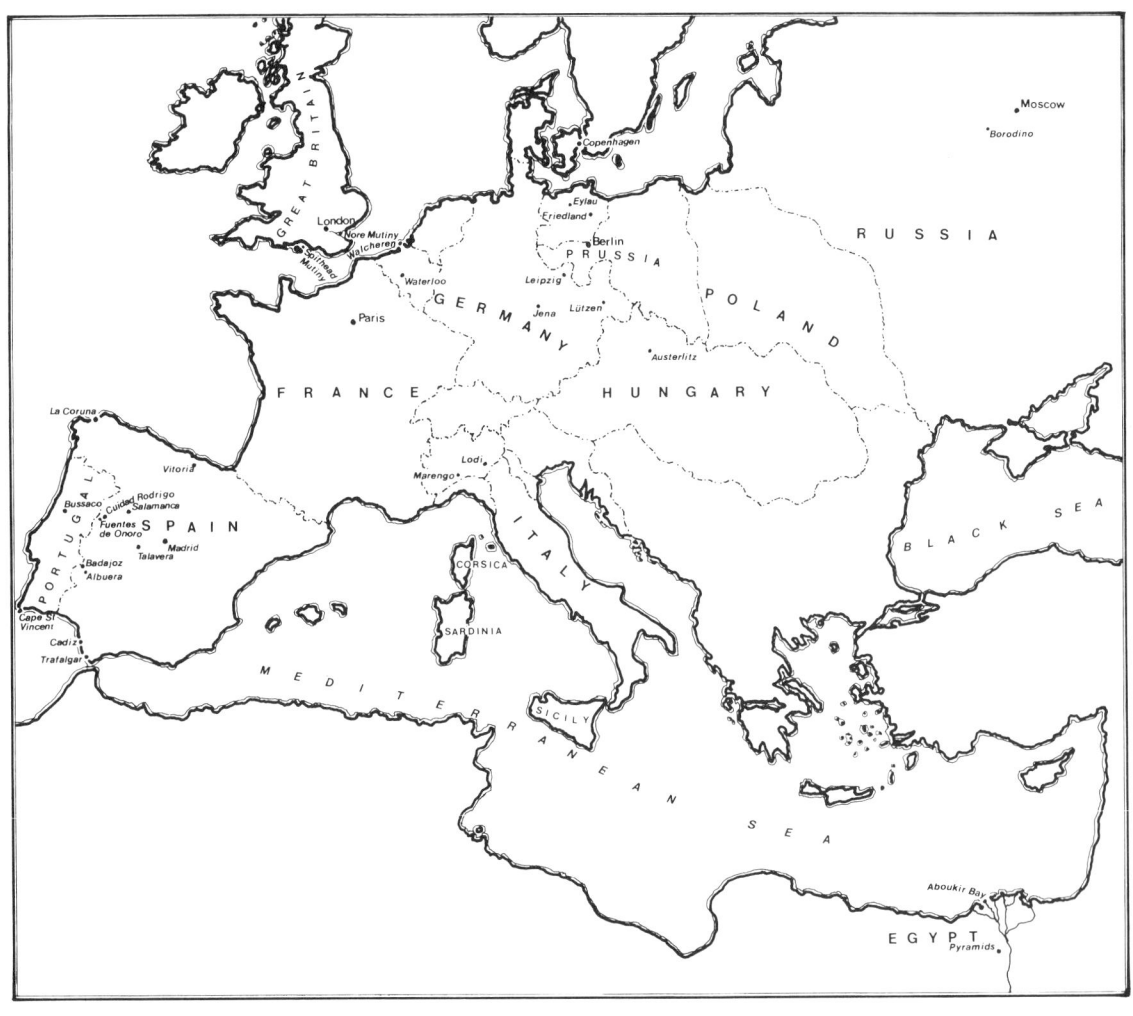

2 The Napoleonic Empire.

Amiens) whilst secretly making plans for an invasion of Britain. Thousands of flat-bottomed boats were made ready to transport his crack troops across the English Channel but, even after hostilities had reopened (Addington's government finally realizing the folly of trusting Napoleon's proffered friendship), the invasion never came. The French fleet could not break the stranglehold which the British navy had over operations in the Channel. Finally, he broke up his invasion camp near Boulogne, where 150,000 men awaited embarkation, and turned his intentions eastwards.

Shortly afterwards, the British Mediterranean Fleet, commanded by Lord Nelson, put an end once and for all to Napoleon's dream of invading Britain when it destroyed the French and Spanish Mediterranean fleets at the Battle of Trafalgar on 21 October 1805.

Thereafter, Napoleon sought to bring Britain to her knees by destroying her foreign trade. In 1806 he issued the Berlin Decrees forbidding all countries under his control to trade with Britain, or accept foods from any ship that had visited a British port. Britain retaliated by claiming the right to seize any ships believed to be bound for French ports; this led to bad feeling developing between Britain and the United States of America, which culminated in a short, but bitter, war between the two countries (1812-14).

Napoleon's decision to invade Russia in the summer of 1812, and his subsequent retreat

3 "A Stoppage to a Stride over the Globe", a patriotic cartoon of 1803 which shows Napoleon straddling the globe, interrupted in his triumphal progress by "Little Johnny Bull".

from Moscow through the bleak mid-winter snows, cost the lives of some 450,000 French troops and, ultimately, cost Napoleon his Empire. By the winter of 1813 Wellington's Penninsular army was battling its way doggedly through Spain and towards the French border (which it finally crossed early in 1814), and the armies of Britain's allies were closing in for the kill from the east. Napoleon abdicated in 1814, and was banished to the island of Elba. The "Little Corsican" had finally been put in his place: the Congress of Vienna set out to restore some kind of order and stability to the European political scene. Then news came that Napoleon was once again on French soil and raising an army, having made one of the most remarkable comebacks in history.

The Battle of Waterloo, described by the Duke of Wellington, commander of the allied army, as "the nearest run thing you ever saw in your life", finally sealed Napoleon's fate. He was exiled to St Helena, and there died in 1821.

So, Napoleon had finally been brought to book, and Britain had played a notable role in his defeat. Despite setbacks her landforces and navy had proved their worth: Nelson and Wellington were national heroes (the former posthumously), and the famous victories at Trafalgar and Waterloo generated intense national pride. After almost a quarter of a century of being at war, the British people could look forward to a peaceful future. They could also look back on the war years and count the cost.

The battles had been fought by professional soldiers and seamen (though it is doubtful if the "pressed" men saw themselves in that light), who accepted the risk of death in battle as a professional hazard. So it had always been. However, what was new about this war was the effect it had on the lives of the British people who remained at home, and who, in the past, had been scarcely touched by foreign wars.

As G.M. Trevelyan in his *English Social History* observes:

Coming at a critical moment in our social development, the long war was a grave misfortune with its violent disturbances of economic life, and its mood of 'anti-Jacobin' reaction against all proposals for reform and all sympathy with the claims and sufferings of the poor — the war formed the worst possible environment for the industrial and social changes then in rapid progress.

The war touched the lives of everyone, from whatever social class, but those who suffered most were those who had least. To pay for the war William Pitt the Younger, and subsequent Prime Ministers, imposed taxes. In 1798 income tax was introduced for all men who earned more than £60 per year. Then in 1803 heavy additional taxes were imposed on beer, wine, tea, sugar and other commodities.

Further tax increases followed annually. By 1806 income tax stood at 10 per cent, and the tax on tea was raised to 96 per cent of its value. This trend continued throughout the war years, causing the most suffering to the families of ordinary working men who, though they did not earn enough to pay income tax, still had to pay the increased taxes on food and manufactured goods.

Hardest hit of all were the families of farm workers who, despite the growth of population in the industrial towns, made up the largest section of the population. Poorly paid and often ill-housed, they were severely affected by the frequent, steep rises in the price of bread, especially during the years of Napoleon's blockade which cut off additional grain supplies from the Continent. During the war years the poor could not be shielded from the effects of a bad harvest. Landowners and farmers made hefty profits, but did nothing to ease the sufferings of their workers, who were kept on low wages. Many had already been adversely affected by the advent of the "enclosure" system, losing their rights of using the common pasture for their animals. The result was widespread poverty and consequent hunger and deprivation. At Speenhamland in Berkshire, in 1795, the local magistrates sought to help the situation by introducing what they termed an Allowance System, whereby labourers who earned less than a basic minimum wage, and had a family, were given a supplement from the poor rates. The system soon spread to other rural areas. Unfortunately, though humane in conception, it created more problems than it solved, since it encouraged farmers to refuse to raise their workers' wages, in the knowledge that parish relief would make up the deficiency.

Many agricultural workers drifted to the growing industrial towns in search of a living wage, but industrial workers were also facing hard times, except in those industries which

4 Gillray's savage cartoon showing William Pitt (The Younger) and his colleagues in the government feasting at a time when the price of bread had risen dramatically because of a shortage of wheat.

5 On 28 April 1812 William Horsfall, a Yorkshire mill-owner who had defied the Luddites' threats, was shot dead. Later three Luddites were hanged at York for his murder, along with 14 others.

serviced the war effort. Especially badly hit were the cotton workers of Lancashire and Cheshire, who were wholly dependent on foreign trade: during the years of the war with the United States (1812-14) little raw cotton was imported, and unemployment was exceptionally high.

The winter of 1808-9 had caused great suffering amongst the poor, but the bleakest period was in 1811-1812. Poor harvests and Napoleon's blockade combined to create severe crises: exports fell to record low levels, imports were severely restricted, and the price of bread rose sharply. Short-time working became the norm for those who managed to retain their jobs, and thousands of workers lost their jobs completely. Civil unrest

6 This picture of the interior of a cellar near St Giles, London, shows that poverty was not confined to rural areas.

followed. Hunger strikes were followed by outbreaks of machine-breaking and factory-burning, initially in Nottinghamshire amongst the angry and disaffected framework knitters, but soon spreading to the wool cloth croppers of Yorkshire and the cotton weavers of Lancashire and Cheshire. Though their exact grievances differed, they were united in a determination to discourage the use of the new labour-saving machinery which they believed threatened their livelihoods by producing cheap but substandard cloth and stockings. The machine-breakers were known collectively as the "Luddites", after their mysterious, legendary "leader" Ned, or "King", Ludd, whose signature appeared on early threatening letters, and whose name became a rallying cry for the disaffected workers.

The government responded by making frame-breaking a capital offence, and by sending large numbers of troops to "police" the areas effected by Luddite disturbances. The Luddites' bitterness and frustration grew, and deaths followed on both sides. The situation grew uglier by the month until in January 1813, 64 men were brought to trial in York Castle: the savagery of the sentences (17 men sentenced to death, seven to be deported) shocked all but the most determined of the Luddites' opponents, but it chastened the communities from which the Luddites drew their support, and the heart went out of the movement. The message was simple:

7 The London-to-Brighton stagecoach, known as *The Comet*, depicted on its way through the Sussex countryside.

machines had come to stay, and men must either adapt or starve. They adapted, but never forgave. The Class war had arrived.

Remarkably, despite set-backs during this war-time period, which saw so much suffering amongst the poor, Britain's economy not only remained strong but positively prospered. The early decades of the Industrial Revolution had created an industrial base which was capable not only of sustaining the country's economy through 22 years of war but also of expanding rapidly.

Britain emerged from the wars not only victorious, but richer and more productive. Though her trade with the Continent had been badly effected by Napoleon's blockade, her trade with the rest of the world, especially India and South America, had increased dramatically, her merchant tonnage rising from one to two-and-a-half million.

The advent of steam power had enabled many of Britain's developing industries, especially iron, to enlarge dramatically. As J.R. Edwards in *English History: 1815-1839* notes:

New inventions worked cumulatively to speed up the rate of change. The use of coal increased the output of iron, the larger output of iron cheapened the cost of machinery, cheaper machines lessened the expense of coal-mining.

Despite the Luddites' opposition and the lack of raw materials during the war with the United States, the cotton textile industry was also expanding as it changed from a cottage to a factory industry. In 1803 Horrocks of Stockport created a version of Cartwright's power loom which revolutionized production methods. As industrial productivity increased, better roads were needed to transport the goods. Thomas Telford and Robert McAdam, rival road engineers, provided them.

Communications in general improved greatly during this period, and those wealthy enough to afford it travelled more widely and comfortably in the improved stage-coaches which plied their trade across the British countryside.

Above all, despite, and at times because of, the bitter struggle with Napoleon's France it was a period of extraordinary inventiveness. Arthur Bryant in *The Age of Elegance* names, with characteristic relish, many of the principal inventors and inventions of the period:

Rennie, the millwright's apprentice who drained the Lincolnshire fens and built docks and iron bridges; weavers and machinists like Crompton and Thomas Johnson who, backed by their employers, made lovely Lancashire the economic cornerstone of the world; the Engineers, Bramah – a village carpenter's boy – Maudslay, Roberts and Whitworth; Trevithick, the Cornish giant, and George Stephenson, the Northumberland collier's son who laid the foundation of the railway age. Steam-power to raise water and coal, and drive engines, ships and vehicles . . . gas to light streets, shops and houses; safety lamps, to prevent explosions in mines; water-closets instead of foul-smelling privies; wooden-legs with elastic springs to reproduce the motions of nature . . . were all, in their different modes, manifestations of the tireless British will to tame nature for amenity and social betterment and grow rich in the process.

The new century had brought with it a new vision of the future, a driving, shaping creative energy which would soon transform Britain into the richest and most powerful nation on earth – precisely what Napoleon had sought, and failed, to achieve for France on the battlefields of Europe.

Manners, Morals And Monarchy

The years 1793 to 1815, then, were years of transformation and change; they were also years of contrast and extremes. For while children starved in the streets of rural villages, the Prince of Wales and his retinue lived lives of wanton extravagance and self-indulgence in London or his favourite new watering-hole, Brighton (see pages 13–16). The Prince had many redeeming features, but in significant areas of national life he set a poor example, which did little to strengthen the position of the monarchy, already weakened by the King's mental disorder and unstable behaviour. The war years required that every citizen should tighten his belt, not loosen it to accommodate a belly swollen by gluttony and excess.

The simple fact was that throughout the war years the denizens of high society in the capital and the wealthy landowners in the country continued to enjoy their pleasures as they

9 (above) A dedicated follower of fashion: a Regency "dandy" steps out elegantly, dressed rather more exuberantly than his mentor "Beau" Brummell considered fitting.

8 (below) The Prince of Wales takes 'A Morning Ride' with two lugubrious companions, pursued by a young groom with a highly original running style.

10 *A Sparring Match at the Fives Court* by Cruikshank (1813). The two pugilists here are wearing gloves, although contests were more usually fought with bare knuckles.

always had; they were irked by the introduction of income tax but not seriously inconvenienced. They followed the latest fashions (mostly set by Beau Brummell, see pages 17–21) with a keen eye, spending freely on clothes and accessories. They ate and drank to excess; they gambled at such gaming clubs as White's or Crockford's; they "followed the turf" and attended bare-knuckle prize-fights; they visited the theatre to see John Philip Kemble and Sarah Siddons, or William Betty, the child prodigy known as the Young Roscius. They built and furnished their town and country houses in the latest styles.

As Arthur Bryant observes "to live expensive and elegant" had become the aim for those who could afford it. It was a golden age for style and, as he continues, "the summum bonum of style was the dandy", typified by the "Prince of Dandies", George "Beau" Brummell who set the fashion in gentlemen's attire for a whole generation before being forced to flee the country to avoid his creditors. Meanwhile, the great ladies of fashionable London society presided regally over their balls and grand parties (known as "routs").

This ostentatious enjoyment of wealth was not confined to London society: the landed gentry were themselves enjoying a heyday. Their great passion was for "improving" their estates, following the advice of such respected landscape gardeners as Humphrey Repton. By the turn of the century the revival of the "Gothic" style was becoming increasingly evident, with a consequent fascination for the picturesque. A visit to Bath "to take the waters" or to London "for the season" was a virtually compulsory part of the social round: it was necessary to "see and be seen", to catch up on the latest fashions and gossip and perhaps arrange a suitable match for an eligible daughter.

The middle-class town-dwellers tended to ape their social "betters", as Jane Austen so tellingly portrayed in her novels (see pages 21–25). Though she satirized the follies and foibles of upper middle-class provincial life, with its smugness and petty snobberies, she was at pains to emphasize the goodness and charm of its essentially cultivated and leisured mode of living. Jane Austen used her "leisure" time to write her novels; unfortunately far too many young ladies of her class suffered from extreme boredom. They frittered away their time doing little or nothing useful to themselves or others, reading Gothic novels or the risqué poetry of the "mad, bad and dangerous to know" Lord Byron, which they borrowed from the circulating libraries, and dreaming of wild, untamed passions quite out of place in their circumscribed lives of decorous routine (read Jane Austen's *Northanger Abbey*). Byron's much-publicized love affair with Lady Caroline Lamb in 1815 made him unacceptable to London society (confirming its growing reputation for hypocrisy) and he left England, never to return from what were, in every sense, the warmer climes of the Mediterranean.

The extravagances and excesses, the hypocrisy and self-delusion of the time disturbed such Christian moralists as William Wilberforce and Hannah More ("the old bishop in petticoats" as William Cobbett called her), who called for a moral reformation in the leaders of society, so that those lower down the social ladder might have a wholesome example to follow. Wealthy, well-connected and influential, Wilberforce and his Evangelical friends sought to do for the rich what Wesley and Methodism had done for the poor. Committed members of the Church of England, they preached the need for sobriety, self-discipline and spiritual renewal founded on bible study and personal "holiness". Remembering the Evangelical influence of his youth G.W.E. Russell recalled,

an abiding sense of religious responsibility, a self-sacrificing energy in works of mercy, an evangelistic zeal, an aloofness from the world, and a level of saintliness in daily life such as I do not expect to see realised on earth again.

It is therefore unsurprising that Wilberforce was also the great champion of the movement for the abolition of slavery, the great moral crusade of his time. For the best part of 20 years he campaigned tirelessly in Parliament, seeking to win over the hearts and minds of his fellow-Parliamentarians. Finally, he succeeded: "The Bill for the Abolition of The Slave Trade" was passed on 4 February 1807 by a majority of 267 votes. Wilberforce, in achieving what had seemed to many impossible, came to be viewed as both the nation's conscience and its inspiration.

Throughout these years of exertion and profound change Britain's monarch, George III, struggled to cope with the distressing effects of porphyria, a disease which caused him to suffer lengthy periods of apparent derangement; from 1810 onwards he lived in a twilight kingdom reminiscent of Shakespeare's King

11 This diagram (used by Wilberforce to illustrate his case) shows the appallingly cramped conditions endured by slaves on board a typical "slaver".

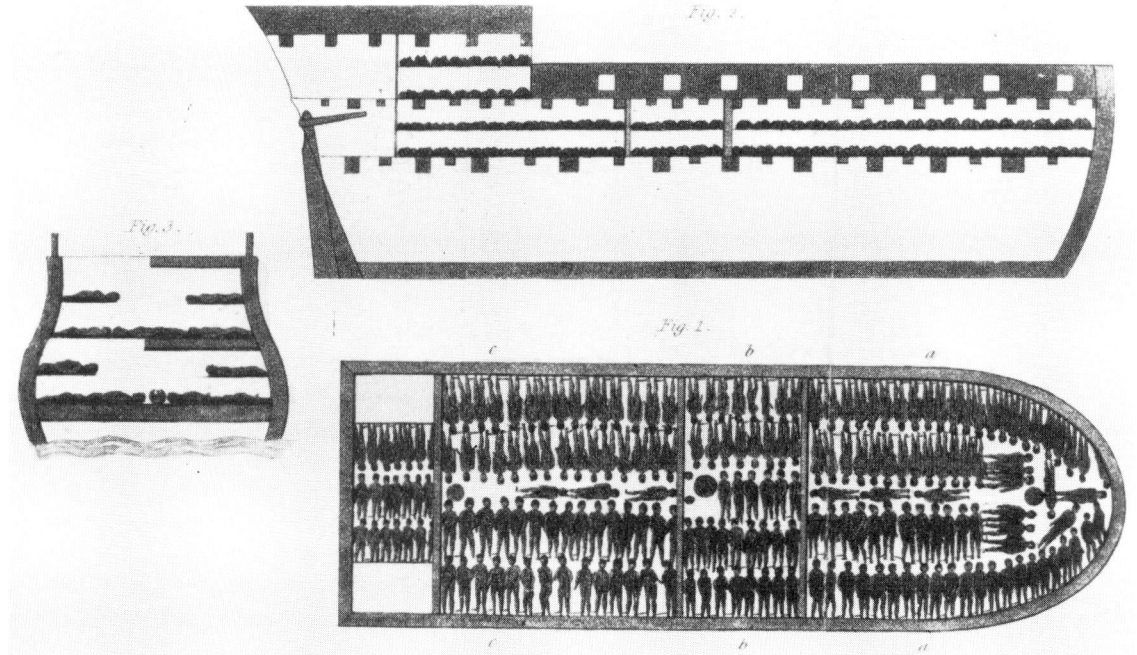

Lear, whom, with his long white hair and beard, he had come to resemble. His responsibilities had long since passed to his eldest son, the Prince of Wales, who was officially appointed Prince Regent in February 1811, and who became, as George IV in 1820, a monarch of very different manners and morals (see pages below, 13–16).

George Augustus Frederick, Prince of Wales (1762-1830)

From an early age the heir to the throne George Augustus Frederick, Prince of Wales, found himself at loggerheads with his father, King George III. The pleasure-loving Prince had little in common with his father's strict Germanic code of behaviour. In adolescence he dutifully endured his military training in Hanover, but as a young man he quickly attracted a reputation for dressing extravagantly, squandering money and falling in love with older women. His father strongly disapproved of his son's "love of dissipation".

Matters were not helped when in 1784 he fell in love with the twice-widowed Maria Fitzherbert, to whom he was married, in secret, on 21 December 1785. Secrecy was essential for two reasons: since 1772 it had been illegal for any member of the royal family under 25 to marry without the King's consent (which clearly would not be forthcoming) and, more importantly, Maria Fitzherbert was a Roman Catholic. Under the Act of Settlement (1701) no prince who married a Roman Catholic could succeed to the throne of England. Though illegal by Constitutional Law, the marriage was legal by Canon Law, and their relationship was accepted by the Prince's friends and even his brothers and sisters. Contemporary wiseacres soon nicknamed her "Princess Fitz", as they had previously nicknamed him "Prinny". The couple's lifestyle was lavish and extravagant, and the Prince's debts mounted alarmingly. In 1783 Parliament had paid off some £30,000 of his debts, but by 1786 he had built up further debts of over £160,000. The King was furious and the Prince closed down Carlton House

12 The Prince of Wales in his Garter robes, 1799.

(given to him by the King as his main residence), dismissed many of his servants and sold most of his carriages and racing horses.

He spent increasingly more time in the small seaside town of Brighton where, in 1787, he set Henry Holland to work on converting a seafront house he had bought into what became known first as the Marine Pavilion

13 A view of the exotic Royal Pavilion at Brighton.

and, later, after much modification, the exotic Royal Pavilion.

Then, late in 1788, the King began to behave in a manner which suggested to contemporaries incipient madness. Doctor John Knyveton's diary vividly records the illness (now thought to be the severe nervous disease, porphyria):

November 11th: the King is gravely ill in his mind, taken first with mental seizures and hallucinations last month when he attempted to shake hands with an oak tree in Windsor Park, declaring it to be his kinsman, Frederick of Prussia. Opinions in the Faculty as to his chances of recovering are divided.

The Whig politician Charles James Fox proposed that the Prince of Wales act as Regent, but early in 1789 the King seemed to regain the possession of his faculties, and a service of thanksgiving was held on 23 April. For many people the thanksgiving was as much for deliverance from the Prince Regent's outrageous behaviour as it was for the return of the King's wits.

The Prince seemed hugely disgruntled – he had coveted the Regency, and its attendant benefits, both for himself and, he fondly believed, the nation. His disrespectful behaviour and indecorous levity (chewing biscuits) at the thanksgiving service endeared him to no one.

However, he quickly returned to his life of luxurious self-indulgence, at the same time that England was going to war with Napoleon. The Prince attended horse-races and bare-knuckle boxing fights, threw extravagant masked balls, ate and drank too much, and philandered with a series of older women, notably Lady Jersey. His relationship with Maria Fitzherbert was put under great strain, and in 1794 they parted for a time.

By 1795 the Prince's debts were astronomical, in excess of £650,000. In desperation he appealed to his father for help. This time the King was not to be fobbed off with promises of economies, but demanded, in exchange for the payment of his debts and the doubling of his income, that the Prince should agree to marry Princess Caroline of Brunswick. The Prince had no choice but to accept the King's terms, though he had never set eyes on her. When he saw her, he was heard to mutter to the Earl of Malmesbury "Harris, I am not well; pray get me a glass of brandy." It was an inauspicious start, but it set the tone for their future relationship.

They were married on 5 April 1795. For some months afterwards they lived together, but the Prince was soon divising elaborate excuses for avoiding her company. On 7 January 1796 the Princess gave birth to a daughter, Princess Charlotte, but within a few months she and her husband were living apart, each maintaining a separate household. The press ridiculed him mercilessly. To some he was a national joke, to others a national

14 *A Voluptuary Under the Horrors of Digestion.* This cartoon shows that as early as 1792 the Prince of Wales's hedonistic self-indulgence was exciting public ridicule.

liability, his ostentatious self-indulgence an obscenity at a time when his country was at war, and poverty widespread.

The Prince appeared largely indifferent to criticsm of his lifestyle. He had become grossly fat, and frequently behaved, in J.B. Priestley's apt phrase "like a giant child", but in 1800 an improvement in his relationship with Maria Fitzherbert led to some tempering of his excesses. Her influence at least moderated that of his "dandy" friends, like George "Beau" Brummell.

In 1804 the King suffered another relapse: this time the Prince seemed certain to be appointed Regent, but once again the King regained his judgement. The Prince, frustrated, spent increasingly more time resident at the Pavilion in Brighton, which by 1804 had been much altered and extended. Much of the interior had been decorated in the Oriental style, and a block of stables built in the grounds. The Prince took an active personal interest in the creation of his "palace of art" at Brighton. He was a man of sensibility and daring aesthetic taste, devoted to all aspects of the Arts. He enjoyed fine music, and painting and read widely, admiring especially the novels of Jane Austen. He even succeeded in impressing a sceptical Lord Byron with his knowledge of the poetry of the period. It was a side of the Prince that too few people knew, or appreciated. The vast majority only saw, or heard of, or read about, the cost of the Prince's patronage of the Arts, his expenditure on "improving" Carlton House and the Pavilion at Brighton, and his impressive but costly collection of art works. As the war dragged on it seemed less and less forgiveable.

In 1810 Princess Amelia, the King's youngest and best-loved daughter died of consumption at the age of 27; distraught with grief, he rapidly lost touch with reality. This time a Regency was inevitable and on 5 February 1811 the Prince of Wales finally, at the age of 49, became Prince Regent.

The Prince was determined to show the nation that he was taking his responsibilities seriously. Ironically it was the Prince's most enthusiastic supporters, the Whigs, who were the most disappointed in him. They naturally expected immediate political promotion, but the Prince, anxious for continuity and stability, chose to retain the Tory Government of Spencer Perceval. As time passed it became clear that the Prince, now that he was in a position of responsibility, was growing steadily more sympathetic to the Tory viewpoint. Many Whig politicians felt betrayed and never forgave him.

1812 was a testing year, with the assassination of the Prime Minister, Spencer Perceval, the beginnings of the Luddite troubles and a renewal of hostilities with the United States. To widespread criticism he appointed as Prime Minister the shrewd and under-rated Lord Liverpool.

In 1813 the tide turned in the war against

Napoleon with news of Wellington's successes in Spain, and Britain at last had something to celebrate. Although the Prince Regent's step hardly grew lighter, he seemed generally more relaxed and expansive. While he still had many critics and enemies there were many others who were beginning to recognize and respect his good qualities. When, in 1813, he severed his friendship with Beau Brummell this seemed to signal the end of an era of dalliance for the Prince.

In 1814 Napoleon was finally brought to book. The combined armies of Britain, Austria, Prussia and Russia had forced him to capitulate, abdicate, and accept exile on the island of Elba near Corsica. The shadow of war was at last lifted from the British people. There was universal rejoicing, the climax of which was the visit to Britain in June of Tsar Alexander I of Russia, King Frederick of Prussia and Prince Metternich representing the Emperor of Austria. The Prince Regent was determined to impress them, particularly Tsar Alexander. He arranged a series of sumptuous banquets and visits to places of interest. Wherever the Tsar went he was cheered to the skies; by contrast, the Prince Regent was frequently booed and jeered. To make matters worse the Tsar had taken a dislike to him and treated him with ill-concealed contempt. It was all greatly upsetting. As Alan Parker in his biography *George IV* comments:

The Prince was soon in the lowest of spirits. He had hoped to bask momentarily in the reflected glory of victory: he found instead that his image was distorted, as though by some mocking mirror.

By the time his guests finally departed from England the Prince was "worn out with fuss, fatigue and rage".

Fortunately with the return to England of the victorious Duke of Wellington, the Prince Regent had a second opportunity to display his talent for creating lavish spectacle. On the night of 1 August, after a day in which there were elaborate celebrations for both Peace with France and the Centenary of the Hanoverian Succession, Hyde Park, St James's Park and Green Park were turned into a blazing fairyland by a firework display, as the essayist Charles Lamb describes:

the fireworks were splendid — the Rockets in clusters, in trees and all shapes, spreading about like young stars in the making, floundering about in Space (like unbroken horses) till some of Newton's calculations should fix them, ...

For once few begrudged the expense.

The year ended with the Congress of Vienna. The Prince Regent sent Lord Castlereagh and the Duke of Wellington to represent the British interest. All seemed to be going smoothly when Napoleon astounded the world by escaping from Elba and returning to France. The Battle of Waterloo followed. During the crisis the Prince Regent showed a greater coolness in the face of Napoleon's renewed threat than many of his fellow European monarchs. Fortunately, his faith in the Duke of Wellington's abilities proved well founded.

After Waterloo, the Prince received an extraordinary letter from Napoleon, who was then seeking refuge in the port of Rochefort:

Pursued by the factions which divide my country and by the hostility of the greatest European powers I have ended my political career and I come . . . to seat myself at the hearth of the British people. I put myself under the protection of its laws, which I claim from Your Royal Highness as the strongest, most consistent and most generous of my foes.

The Prince Regent was greatly moved by the appeal but knew that he could not, safely, offer Napoleon the asylum he requested. He must have reflected, ruefully, that his greatest enemy had paid him a compliment of which few of his own countrymen would have thought him worthy.

The Prince Regent was crowned King George IV on 19 July 1821 and died on 26 June 1830.

Beau Brummell (1778-1840)

For more than 15 years George "Beau" Brummell was the dictator and arbiter of male dress and appearance in fashionable society. Even the Prince of Wales looked to him for guidance, and was known "to blubber when told that Brummell did not like the cut of his coat", as the poet and satirist Tom Moore drily records. His position as the most influential of London's "Dandies" seemed unassailable. Yet in 1816, hopelessly in debt, he was forced to flee the country and seek refuge in France. He never again set foot on British soil, and died in poverty and degradation. His story says much about the fickleness of fortune in the so-called Age of Elegance.

George Bryan Brummell was born in June 1778. His father was the Private Secretary to the Prime Minister and, as such, an influential man. In 1786 George and his brother, after a happy childhood at their country house home, were dispatched to Eton. From the first he was a general favourite; his popularity with both staff and fellow-students shielded him from the more brutal excesses of Eton life, so he was free to develop the image which, if to some extent a pose when he was at Eton, soon became the essence of the man himself when he launched himself upon the London social scene. The key to this persona was an extreme fastidiousness about matters of dress and personal hygiene, coupled with a highly-developed sense of social decorum and good manners. Even as a young man George Brummell had an individuality of style which others sought to copy. A contemporary of his noted

the anxiety with which he eschewed the dirty streets on a rainy day, his white stock [collar] with a bright gold buckle behind, and the measured dignity of his step. His language, dress and deportment were always in perfect keeping.

In 1794, at his father's request, "Buck"

15 Beau Brummell as a young man.

Brummell (as he had been nicknamed) left Eton and took up residence at Oriel College, Oxford. It was his father's hope that he would, one day, become a politician. But when in 1794 his father died (exactly a year after the death of his mother) he felt free to follow his own inclinations. He left Oxford after one term and, on the offer of the Prince of Wales, took up an army commission, a cornetcy, in the 10th Light Dragoons, then the most fashionable, if not the most active, regiment in the British Army. Clearly, he had come to the Prince's notice, probably on the recommendation of one of his late father's Whig friends.

He joined his regiment in Hounslow and from there he went on frequent jaunts to London. His first service for his future friend and patron, his regimental Colonel-in-Chief,

the Prince of Wales, was in April 1795 when he was a member of the regimental escort sent to meet the Prince's future wife, Princess Caroline of Brunswick when she landed in England, and escort her to St James's Palace.

Three days later he was in attendance on the Prince at his wedding in the Chapel Royal: a great honour for a youth of 17, even one so self-possessed and charming as George Brummell. A contemporary describes something of his extraordinary fascination:

the just proportions of his form were remarkable; his hand was particularly well-shaped; his face was rather long, and complexion fair; his hair light brown. His head was well shaped, the forehead being unusually high. His countenance indicated that he possessed considerable intelligence, and his mouth betrayed a strong disposition to indulge in sardonic humour. His eyebrows were equally expressive with his mouth, and while the latter was giving utterance to something very good-humoured or polite, the former, and the eyes themselves, which were grey and full of oddity, could assume an expression that gave additional point to his humourous or satirical remarks. His voice was very pleasing.

16 Here Beau Brummell acts as usher to the Prince of Wales and his retinue.

Later in 1795 the 10th Light Dragoons moved to Brighton where the Prince could satisfy more readily his love of military display. Soon after, the newly-promoted Lieutenant Brummell fell from his horse and broke his nose; the resulting somewhat upturned nose gave him a disdainful air which many found off-putting but with which he pronounced himself delighted.

Over the next few years Lieutenant Brummell was seen increasingly in the Prince's company: he had rapidly become a favoured companion of the "Prince of Pleasure" (as J.B. Priestley named him), who immoderately admired his elegant dress-sense and impeccable manners. In 1796 Lieutenant Brummell was promoted to Captain (almost certainly money changed hands), though it was said that he could scarcely recognize the men in his own troop, so little time did he allot to his military duties.

In 1797 he legally came of age, and inherited a large capital sum left him by his father. He was now financially independent and, but for the inconvenience of his military duties, free to make his mark in fashionable society. In 1798 his regiment was ordered to Manchester to restore law and order after local rioting had disturbed the peace. For Brummell it was the ultimate inconvenience; he wittily announced to friends that he was "not prepared to go on foreign service", and set off to beg the Prince to prevent it. Hubert Cole, in his biography *Beau Brummell* records (if Brummell's own anecdote is to be believed) that Brummel ended his plea by announcing that he had decided to sell out, to which the Prince replied

"Oh by all means, Brummell. Do as you please!"

Freed from his army responsibilities, "Buck" Brummell set about single-mindedly, and with painstaking attention to detail, redefining the notion of what it was to be a gentleman. "Buck" Brummell was quickly transformed into "Beau" Brummell, the archetypal dandy.

It was Brummell's scrupulous attention to personal hygiene which first attracted notice. Every morning he spent several hours preparing himself for the day ahead (or rather the remainder of it): he encouraged stories that he regularly bathed in a mixture of water, milk and eau de cologne, just as he later encouraged the notion that he cleaned his boots with champagne. The stories were probably true, but the important thing for "Beau" Brummell was that people were prepared to believe them. If he was to be copied, he had first to be noticed, so he made quite certain that he was a frequent topic of conversation in the drawing rooms of the gossip-loving great.

Soon, his views about what clothes to wear, and how to wear them, were discussed everywhere in fashionable society, and followed slavishly by the younger generation of *beaux* (and many older ones), eager to be recognized as dandies. Interestingly, though the term "dandy" suggests sartorial extravagance to modern ears, the very reverse was the case. "Beau" Brummell, the "high priest of dandyism", (as J.B. Priestley calls him) despised extravagance of dress, and insisted that a gentleman should wear well-cut and fitted clothes made not of silks or satins or brocades but from quietly-coloured cloth of the finest quality. His maxim was:

17 A somewhat unflattering drawing of Beau Brummell in conversation with the Duchess of Rutland; from Gronow's *Reminiscences*.

If John Bull turns round to look after you, you are not well dressed: but either too stiff or too tight, or too fashionable!

Another favourite saying was "no scents, but plenty of clean linen, country bleached [i.e. by sun and air]".

Brummell's rejection of the flamboyant, French-influenced, style of dress fashionable in the 1770s and 1780s, in favour of the clean-lined elegance of his own style created the look of a whole generation of wealthy young, fashion-conscious men. As Arthur Bryant in *The Age of Elegance* observes:

A dandy was a formidable figure – the wide-brimmed glossy hat, always new, the spotless, white-starched cravat so tight and high that the wearer could scarcely look down or turn his head . . . the exquisitely cut coat worn wide-open to display the waistcoat of buff, yellow or rose and the snowy embroidered cambric shirt; the skin-tight pantaloons, or "inexpressibles" gathered up into a wasp's waist and bulging like a succession of petticoats under the stays; the fobs, jewels, chains and spotless gloves; the white-thorn [hawthorn] cane . . . the wonderfully made boots whose shine rivalled the cuirasses of the Life Guards . . .

Beau Brummell's extraordinary influence on the fashions of the period stemmed from two sources: his own cool self-assurance in what he wore and how he behaved, and the hold he very quickly achieved over the Prince of Wales, who was not only fascinated by his audacity, but intrigued by his ideas. Brummell continued to influence the Prince's dress-sense throughout the years of their friendship: he was never entirely successful in eradicating the Prince's love of ostentation, but he kept it in check.

Throughout the first decade of the new century Brummell was regularly seen at the Prince's side. He was a "figure" in fashionable society, renowned as much for his audacious impertinence as for his elegant appearance. At a particularly grand ball he is supposed to have said to the Duchess of Rutland:

In Heaven's name my dear Duchess what is the meaning of this extraordinary back of yours? I declare I must put you on a backboard; you must positively walk out of the room backwards, that I mayn't see it!

His disdainful manner with those he found

18 A gaming room at Brooks's Club in London (1808).

tedious could be highly provoking, and he made as many enemies as friends, though it is clear that he had a great gift for friendship. In 1811 this was put to the test when it became clear that his friendship with the Prince was cooling rapidly. The Prince was growing increasingly resentful of the centrality of "Beau" Brummell's position in fashionable society and he came to feel that he was being elbowed out of the position as arbiter of taste that he felt was rightfully his. Brummell, by temperament an ascetic, grew increasingly disgusted with the Prince's gross self-indulgence, which was causing him to grow excessively fat. Gradually they drifted apart until each had little good to say of the other. Disparaging remarks made by Brummell about the Prince were reported back to him by those who rejoiced in the breakdown of their relationship, the most hurtful of which was Brummell's observation to Colonel McMahon, "I made him what he is, and I can unmake him." Such an arrogant remark smacked of insolent pride before a fall.

By 1813 Brummell had been gambling heavily for some time; his estrangement from the Prince, now Prince Regent, had adversely affected his ability to get the credit which had hitherto been essential in the maintenance of his position in society, and he looked to gambling to enable him to continue to live beyond his means. 1812 was a bad year for his finances, his losses having outweighed his gains, but in 1813 he began to win large sums of money, and to celebrate he set about organizing, with friends, an extravagant masked ball. Pointedly, he did not invite the Prince Regent who, hearing of his exclusion, simply wrote to announce that he would attend. Grudgingly, an invitation was sent.

On the night of the ball the hosts lined up to receive their guests. When the Prince arrived he turned his back on Brummell. Out of the shocked silence caused by this act of gross bad manners came Brummell's cold clear voice, "Ah Alvaney, who is your fat friend?" The Prince was cut to the quick: he passed on into the ballroom, and out of the life of "Beau" Brummell.

Brummell, for his part, was unconcerned; he had his position in society, and his own circle of friends, many of whom idolized him. What did concern him was that, in 1814, his luck at the gambling tables once more turned. He began to lose heavily and to meet his debts he took out annuities at a crippling rate of interest.

The crisis came in 1816. His debts had mounted steeply, and he began to lose the confidence of his creditors. He determined to cut his losses and leave the country. On the night of 30 March he sailed in secret for France, never to return. It was the end of an era. He died in France 24 years later, wretched, penniless and forgotten, in the asylum of the Bon Sauveur, Caen.

Jane Austen (1775-1817)

Jane Austen was born on 16 December 1775 in the North Hampshire village of Steventon, where her father the Rev. George Austen was Rector. She was the seventh of eight children.

At the age of six Jane and her only sister Cassandra (two years her elder) were sent away to a boarding school; there they nearly died of "putrid fever" (probably diptheria) before being rescued by their outraged mother. After a brief time at another school, their father, anxious at their lack of intellectual development, brought them home and taught them himself. So the two sisters grew up at Steventon sharing the same room, interests, pastimes, daily routine and sources of amusement. They were inseparable

19 Jane Austen. A pencil and watercolour miniature painted by Cassandra Austen in 1801.

companions. As their mother frequently observed,

If Cassandra was going to have her head cut off, Jane would insist on sharing her fate.

A man of discriminating literary taste, George Austen encouraged his children to make full use of his extensive library, and Jane, in particular, became an avid reader of contemporary novels, enjoying especially those of Samuel Richardson and Fanny Burney as she grew into adolescence.

Between the years 1787 and 1793 Jane Austen filled three large notebooks with her own youthful writings which, it is clear, were from the outset family property, read aloud to and shared with whoever was available. She was encouraged in particular by her father, who must have been gratified to find her writing her first full-length book at the age of 14. Entitled *Love and Friendship*, and written in the form of a correspondence, it is a delightfully tongue-in-cheek "send-up" of the sort of romantic novel popular at the time, in which emotionally self-indulgent heroines swoon and "run mad" whenever their passions are excited, and posturing heroes risk all for love.

The next decade, the last of the eighteenth century, saw Jane Austen develop from a 15-year old girl with literary ambitions, who delighted to amuse her readers, into a 25-year old woman who, with completed novels in her drawer, found in her writing the chief solace, joy and interest of her life.

It was a decade that saw many comings and goings at Steventon and changes in the Austen family. In 1791 Jane's 12-year old brother Charles left home to join his brother Francis in the Royal Navy. Later that year Francis returned home after an absence of two years sailing with the Fleet in the East Indies, and Henry was made a Lieutenant in the Oxfordshire militia. Two of her other brothers were married during that time, and two others had children. So the thoughts of the two sisters must have frequently run on courtship and marriage, setting up home and having babies: and, of course, the prerequisite for all of these was an eligible man for a husband. In 1795 her sister Cassandra became engaged, and Jane herself became romantically involved with the Irish nephew of a family friend, Tom Lefroy. Letters from Jane to the temporarily absent Cassandra, are full of light-hearted, and often tongue-in-cheek references to the progress of the courtship. For example,

He (Tom Lefroy) is a very gentleman like, good-looking, pleasant young man, I assure you. But, as to our ever having met, except at the last three balls, I cannot say much; for he is so excessively laughed at about me at Ashe, that he is ashamed of coming to Steventon, and ran away when we called upon Mrs Lefroy a few days ago.

The attachment continued in a low-key, half-humorous way throughout 1796, until it began to show signs of taking a more serious turn, at which point Tom Lefroy's father summoned him home to Ireland. Jane Austen never saw him again.

However, disappointed as she must have been, she had much to occupy her mind. Since early 1795 she had been at work on a full-length novel, again in letter form, which she had entitled "Elinor and Marianne", and in 1796 she had begun work on a new novel, written in narrative form, and provisionally titled "First Impressions".

In February 1797 tragic news reached the Austen family: Cassandra's fiancé Thomas Fowle had caught yellow fever in San Domingo in the East Indies, and died. Cassandra bore her grief with fortitude but she was deeply distressed, and her sister's loving concern was never more gratefully received. Despite this Jane had completed *First Impressions* which gave her great satisfaction, though she was bitterly disappointed when the novel was rejected, unread, by the publishers Messrs Cadell, to whom her father had sent the manuscript. Undaunted, she began work in 1798 on a new novel, initially titled "Lady Susan", later published as *Northanger Abbey*, which drew heavily on her recent experience of the Bath social scene, and her reading of the Gothic novels of Mrs Radcliffe, and which satirized both.

1799 ended somewhat dramatically with Jane's aunt, the forbidding Jane Leigh-Perrot, being accused of shop-lifting (an offence which could carry the death penalty). However, she was acquitted and the drama did not have tragic consequences. Then, in November 1800 her father astonished everyone by announcing his intention to retire and move his household to Bath.

The family duly moved in the early summer of 1801. Initially, Jane felt rootless and homesick for the Steventon countryside, but she was a realist, and practical enough to know that she had to make the best of what she could not change. And Bath had its compensations. As David Cecil in *A Portrait of Jane Austen* observes:

she found much to entertain her there. Bath had ceased to be as fashionable as it had been 50 years earlier: the smart set of London had begun to prefer Regency Brighton. But Jane Austen's own world, the world of the country gentry, remained loyal to Bath. It was to Bath they crowded for some urban relaxation and amuse-

20 Camden Place, Bath.

ment; by night at the theatre or at balls and concerts at the Upper or Lower Assembly Rooms; by day, meeting their friends at the Pump Room, going on expeditions to neighbouring beauty spots, walking the streets to inspect the new fashions at the milliner's or new songs at the music shop, or new novels at the bookseller's.

Later that summer, the family went to Sidmouth for a holiday. There, it seems, Jane Austen fell in love with a handsome and intelligent young clergyman. Sadly after some two or three weeks he was forced to leave Sidmouth; the next news Jane had of him (some few weeks later) was that he had died suddenly. Her distress must have been intense: even Cassandra, a jealous guard of her sister's best interests, had thought them ideally suited.

A year later in 1802 Jane Austen accepted the marriage proposal of the unexciting but dependable Harris Bigg-Wither, a family friend, but changed her mind overnight and refused him.

Meanwhile she continued to be preoccupied

by her writing. The family had settled at number 4 Sydney Place in Bath, and a degree of order had been restored to her life. In 1803 she sold the manuscript of *Northanger Abbey* to the publisher Thomas Crosby. Unaccountably he chose not to publish the book, which remained in his drawer until 1816, when the Austen family finally bought it back from him. Jane Austen's frustration and demoralization at this second failure to get a book published must have been extreme, but she began work on a new novel, *The Watsons*, which, though she returned to it a number of times, was to remain unfinished at her death.

Then in January 1805 Jane Austen's secure home life was shattered when her father died suddenly. The whole family was heartbroken, and the Austens' affairs were thrown into disarray. All the brothers rallied together to provide a comfortable income for their mother and sisters.

In the autumn of 1806 Mrs Austen and her daughters moved into a spacious house in Southampton with her son Frank Austen and his wife, to cut down on expense. The arrangement proved a happy one, although Jane was never wholly at ease living in a large town, and wrote little or nothing during her time there.

In 1809 Edward Austen offered his mother and sisters the opportunity to move back into the countryside, to a large cottage in the pretty Hampshire village of Chawton. They were all delighted and moved there in July 1809.

The most immediate effect on Jane of this return to the Hampshire countryside she so loved was a renewal of interest in her unpublished novels. She set about writing fresh drafts of both "Elinor and Marianne", which she re-titled *Sense and Sensibility*, and "First Impressions", re-titled *Pride and Prejudice*. She continued this work throughout 1810, whilst, at the same time, taking a major share of the responsibility for running the household. She also took very seriously her responsibilities as aunt to an ever-increasing number of nephews and nieces.

In October 1811, thanks to the good offices of her brother Henry, Jane Austen's *Sense and Sensibility* was finally published by Thomas

21 The title page of Jane Austen's novel *Sense and Sensibility*, on which the author remains anonymous.

Egerton of Whitehall in three volumes. Concerned to retain her anonymity, Jane Austen insisted that the frontispiece should read "By a Lady". The novel sold very satisfactorily, and went into a second edition, earning the author £140.

Though fiercely guarding her anonymity, even from her favourite niece Anna, Jane Austen must have been quietly delighted. During 1811 and 1812 she began work on a brand new novel, *Mansfield Park*, and continued to prepare "Pride and Prejudice" for publication. It was duly published in January 1813, and substantially increased the reputation of its anonymous author.

Though the bulk of her time was spent at Chawton, Jane Austen made a number of trips to London to see Henry (now a widower), and to Godmersham to see Edward and his family, where in the evenings she enjoyed the party atmosphere which often prevailed. She found the new status accorded to her as a middle-aged spinster a matter for wry amusement. She wrote to Cassandra:

By the by as I must leave off being young, I find many *douceurs* in being a sort of chaperone; for I am put on the sofa near the fire and can drink as much wine as I like.

Early in 1814 she began a second new novel, *Emma*, and in May *Mansfield Park* was published and favourably received. By the end of the year the first edition was sold out. It was at this time that Jane Austen entered into lengthy correspondence with her two nieces Fanny Knight and Anna Austen: with Fanny primarily about her affairs of the heart, and with Anna offering practical criticism of the novel she had begun to write. Jane Austen's letters to both nieces are full of good-humoured and sensible suggestions, and are never patronizing: clearly the two young women occupied a special place in her life.

In March 1815 *Emma* was completed and a few months later a new novel *Persuasion* begun. *Emma* was published in December by John Murray; it was dedicated, with his permission, to the Prince Regent, who was an avid reader of her books (though Jane Austen had little good to say of him or his politics).

In 1816 Jane Austen, who had spent much of 1815 nursing her brother Henry through an illness, finished *Persuasion* in August and worked on revising the manuscript of *Northanger Abbey*, which Henry had finally extracted from the recalcitrant publisher Crosby.

By 1817 it was clear that she was seriously ill. Her family decided she must seek the help of the famous Doctor Lyford. On 24 May 1817 she set off for Winchester, where he advised her to stay for treatment: she died six weeks later on 18 July of a disease which was only identified some years after her death (Addison's disease).

Her two novels *Persuasion* and *Northanger Abbey* were published posthumously in 1818, and an unfinished novel *Sanditon* was discovered amongst her papers.

In his diary of 1826 Sir Walter Scott, the author of the highly successful Waverley novels, wrote of her:

That young lady has a talent for describing the involvements and feelings and characters of ordinary life, which is the most wonderful I ever met with . . . the exquisite touch which renders ordinary and common-place things and characters interesting from the truth of the description and the sentiment is denied to me . . . . What a pity such a creature died so young!

Radicalism And Reform

The French Revolution of 1789 was a watershed in world history: the unthinkable had happened, a popular rising had toppled a European monarch and executed him – thereafter anything seemed possible. For the radicals and reformers in Britain it was both an inspiration and a challenge. However, as time passed and reports of the appalling atrocities committed during the Reign of Terror filtered back to Britain, many British radicals grew increasingly uneasy. They were men of conscience who found it difficult to reconcile such wholesale blood-letting with their belief in liberty, equality and fraternity (the ideals of the proclaimed Revolution). There followed a backlash of feeling against the Revolution and its ideas in Britain (where many people had initially welcomed it). The outbreak of hostilities with Revolutionary France in 1793 further weakened their position: popular dislike of so-called "English Jacobins" (as the supporters of the Revolution's ideas were called) grew as the war continued. Radicals and reformers came to be seen as enemies of the state, and were often treated as such, though many were, in reality, committed patriots.

The government, fearing that a revolution

22 "French Liberty and British Slavery". A satirical cartoon by Gillray (1792) compares a half-starved French revolutionary gnawing on cold stringy vegetables with a well-fed English gentleman tucking into a plate of roast beef.

of some kind might break out in Britain, and inspired by the example of the French Revolution, took strict steps to avert it: a reactionary and repressive policy was adopted which restricted personal freedom in the name of the national interest and state security. In 1793 the Aliens Act required all aliens to be registered, and allowed anyone to be arrested and deported if even suspected of spying. Then in 1794, in response to agitation for the extension of the voting franchise by the London Corresponding Societies (an early form of trade union), the government suspended Habeas Corpus, a basic human right protecting people from unjustified arrest, and arrested leading members of the society (who were later acquitted). In 1795 the Treasonable and Seditious Practices Act further extended the definition of treason: it was followed by the Seditious Meetings Act which banned all public meetings not authorized by a local Justice of the Peace.

All these repressive measures were steered through Parliament by William Pitt who, although a libertarian, felt compelled to stifle at birth all disagreement and dissent at home which might adversely affect the war effort overseas. They were also used to make life difficult for those reformers who sought to win better pay and working conditions for agricultural and industrial workers: the Combination Acts of 1799 and 1800 forbade all workers to combine and plan concerted action to improve their lot. A number of these early trade unions were forced to disband, but most continued to operate in secret. They were, in effect, driven "underground". The Combination Acts were not repealed until 1824 when a campaign led by Francis Place finally succeeded in persuading the government to soften its "hard line" approach.

Throughout the war years, despite the constraints of the new laws, men like Francis Place worked hard to further the cause, seeking by discussion and persuasion to achieve a better life for the British working man; but it was not easy, and a number of reformers found themselves imprisoned for their beliefs.

23 Cruikshank's establishment view of the seamen's delegates during the Mutiny at the Nore, one of whom is pictured saying, "Tell him we intend to be masters" as he pours out a canful of grog (a mixture of rum and water).

The government's repressive policy largely succeeded in quelling popular discontent or, at least, the expression of it, but the events of 1797/8 severely jolted Pitt's confidence. In 1797 mutinies in the Navy broke out first at Spithead, and then at the Nore in Kent: both were put down, the former with leniency and a recognition of the justice of the sailors' cause, the latter with severity. Then in 1798 an armed rebellion by nationalist Irishmen, led by Wolfe Tone, created further problems until it was stamped out at Vinegar Hill, despite the presence of French troops fighting on the Irishmen's side.

Later, in 1811-1813, some years after Pitt's death, the Luddite riots caused the government of Lord Liverpool extreme disquiet (see pages 8-9), and led to the home deployment of troops who could, and should, have been used in the struggle against Napoleon.

However, Britain did not undergo a bloody insurrection in the manner of the French Revolution; its monarchy and institutions remained intact. The war, by providing an external enemy, distracted the majority of British people from the problems, inadequacies and injustices within their society. Significantly, after the war ended there was an upsurge of radical agitation which precipitated even harsher repression.

Clearly there were many different causes championed by radicals and reformers during the period of the Napoleonic Wars: many different voices, some loud, some quiet, some heard, some unheard. What united them all was a conviction that a more humane, just and equitable society could be achieved if enough people desired it, and had the courage of their convictions.

William Cobbett (1762-1835)

Never a man to follow a predictable path, William Cobbett stood on its head the adage that men are reformers in their youth and conservatives in their maturity. Up to the age of 44 Cobbett was a pugnacious defender of all that was conservative and reactionary in British politics; he violently opposed the French Revolution, poured scorn on all Radicals and reformers and, when living in America, championed the cause of the British monarchy. Yet in 1807 Cobbett became a powerful radical agitator, espousing the very ideas and causes he had previously attacked with such fierce contempt.

To understand this apparent about-face it is necessary to trace the origins of Cobbett's political and social convictions. Born in 1762, the son of a small farmer and innkeeper, he spent many happy days in his childhood out in the fields of the Vale of Farnham, Surrey, performing simple tasks for his father, as he proudly relates in his autobiography *The Life and Adventures of Peter Porcupine* (1796):

My first occupation was driving the small birds from the turnip-seed, and the rooks from the peas. When first I trudged afield, with my wooden bottle and my satchel swung over my shoulder, I was hardly able to climb the gates and stiles.

He rapidly grew into a robust, healthy, enquiring boy with an adventurous spirit. Fiercely independent and self-willed, he frequently defied his parents and took to the road; on one occasion in 1774, he walked to London to find work in Kew Gardens. Later, in 1782, his wandering spirit took him to Portsmouth (where he attempted to join the Navy) and again to London in 1783 when he found work as a lawyer's clerk.

In 1784 he enlisted in the 54th Regiment of Foot and sailed to Nova Scotia. He was soon promoted to sergeant-major, but when in 1791 he procured his discharge he set out to bring to justice a group of dishonest officers who had "fiddled" the Regimental books for personal gain.

Shortly before the trial was due in the spring of 1792 Cobbett found himself abandoned by the men who had agreed to corroborate his testimony. Disgusted and fearful of reprisals, he sailed for France with his young wife Ann, whom he had married on 5 February 1792. Though initially happy there, he was profoundly disturbed by the horrifying events which marked the beginning of the Reign of Terror, and determined to attempt a fresh start in the New World. So he and his wife took ship for America, landing there in October 1792.

At the outset he made a sparse living from teaching French emigrés to speak English, but his true ambition was to become an able journalist and pamphleteer. In August 1794 he published his first political pamphlet, a vigorous attack on the radical scientist Dr Joseph Priestley, who had recently fled from England after his house had been burned down by a Birmingham mob. It created an immediate controversy, and was frequently reprinted. Cobbett found himself impelled to defend his native land against those American Republicans who sympathized with the ideals and notions of Revolutionary France. Savagely denouncing everybody and everything radical or progressive, he delighted in infuriating his American readers. He even placed portraits of the British Royal family in his shop window "to excite rage in the enemies of Britain". In 1796 he began a monthly tract *The Censor*, but replaced this in 1797 with a daily newspaper which he, archly, called *Peter*

24 A contemporary cartoon depicting Cobbett's flight to France in 1792 when the men who had agreed to confirm his charges in court against dishonest officers in his former regiment let him down at the last minute.

Porcupine's Gazette, since one of his critics had said of him he "pricked his enemies like a porcupine". For the next three years he wrote many articles in his pungent, no-nonsense, aggressive style: naturally he made many enemies, who sought, by every means, to silence him. He was twice brought to trial accused of libel, and after the second case, severely fined. Angry, and a little anxious, in 1800 he decided to return to England where he felt assured of a warm reception from the government of William Pitt.

So it proved. Lionized and made much of, he was invited to edit an official government newspaper. Though tempted, he refused, preferring to retain his independent voice. He would defend government policy but on his own terms, and because he believed it just: he had no intention of becoming a Party hack. In 1801 he started his own daily newspaper, *The Porcupine*, in the pages of which he passionately advocated a vigorous prosecution of the war with France.

In January 1801 Pitt resigned, and was replaced by Henry Addington who, in March 1802, signed the Treaty of Amiens, bringing hostilities with France to an end. Cobbett was appalled. In defiance of public opinion he made his views clearly known, undeterred by the attack of a mob on his London home. When in 1802 the war resumed in response to Napoleon's duplicity, Cobbett became a popular hero, greatly to his contemptuous amusement.

Earlier, in November 1801, *The Porcupine*, run on a financial shoestring, had finally failed. With typical resilience Cobbett had started a weekly journal to replace it. *The Political Register* rapidly achieved a solid readership, eager to know what Cobbett felt about the issues of the day. During the years 1801-1806 his allegiances and sympathies began at first subtly, then more overtly, to change and develop into a new perspective on political and social realities. He was growing increasingly disillusioned with Pitt's political methods and what he called "The Pitt System", or scornfully "The Thing", which he believed represented a conspiracy between the politicians, bankers, merchants and men of property to feather their own nests at the expense of the poor and needy. He described it as:

25 William Cobbett at work on the *Political Register*, his widely-read and influential news-sheet.

The system of upstarts; of lowbred, low-minded sycophants, usurping the stations designed by nature, by reason, by the constitution, and by the interests of the people, to men of high birth, eminent talents or great national services.

To Cobbett's mind the wrong people were governing the country for the wrong reasons, and in the wrong way. And "the people" were suffering. He became convinced that unless there were significant reforms of the political system "The Thing" would triumph and the "Old England" of his childhood and youth would be destroyed for ever. Distrustful of both political parties he later wrote:

The Crown had one party in possession and another in expectancy, while the people had no party at all.

Henceforward he determined to be the People's party himself.

His belief in the need to preserve the best of the old country ways was strengthened by his purchase in 1805 of Botley Farm in Hampshire, where he experimented with modern farming methods but strove to retain the traditional relationship between farmer, labourer and land. He continued to edit *The Political Register* from Botley and, if anything, his journalistic output increased. With the passionate commitment of the convert, he assailed the enemies of change with what Hazlitt called the "mutton-fist" of his prose. The Government, whether that of Pitt (who died in 1806) or his successors, could do little right in Cobbett's eyes: he particularly disliked its replacement of good old-fashioned gold and silver by "worthless paper currency". To Cobbett it was just another example of traditional honesty and integrity being replaced by pragmatism and chicanery.

Frank and fearless as he was, Cobbett made many enemies, and in 1810 he gave them the excuse they needed to exact vengeance when he denounced, in print, the flogging of a group of mutinous soldiers in Ely by some over-zealous German mercenaries. He was tried and found guilty of seditious libel. For two years he continued to edit *The Political Register* from Newgate Prison, steadfastly refusing to moderate his criticisms of Government policies. He emerged in 1812, unrepentant, but facing financial ruin. He was forced to sell his farm at Botley and *Parliamentary Debates*, his publication started in 1804 to record the proceedings of the House. For a time his fortunes were at a low ebb, but he never faltered in his determination to speak the plain truth, and his writing became, more passionately vehement than before.

Among the causes he spoke out for was that of the Luddites: though he abhorred their violence, he understood what had driven them to such extremes. He reminded the government that:

> Measures ought to be adopted, not so much for putting an end to riots, as to prevent the misery out of which they arise.

Between 1812 and 1817 (when he returned for a time to the United States) Cobbett produced some of his most effective journalistic writing, frequently shaking the foundations of Government composure with his accustomed savage indignation.

William Hazlitt, the contemporary essayist, wrote of him:

> He is not only the most powerful political writer of the present day, but one of the best writers in the language. He speaks, and thinks, plain, broad, downright English.

And it was a plain, broad, downright England (the England that he later recorded in his *Rural Rides*, written during the 1820s) that he strove, all his life, to preserve.

He died in 1835, three years after becoming an MP, truculent, bombastic and truthful to the last.

26 A £1 note issued in 1797, an example of the "paper money" which Cobbett so vehemently scorned.

Francis Place (1771-1854)

France Place, known as "the radical tailor of Charing Cross" spent much of his life trying "to promote the welfare of the working people". He was the eldest son of a bailiff of the Marshalsea Court in London. As the eldest, he was permitted some formal education, but he learned most from the London streets. A lively, mischievous boy, he enjoyed escapades and pranks, especially nailing the coats of potential customers to the wooden shutters of pastry shops as they inspected the merchandise. He also took part in the common "amusement" of bullock hunting, when a bullock on its way to the slaughterhouse at Smithfield was chased, teased and tormented by a jeering mob. Later Place attacked such barbarous "pastimes" and doubtless regretted his own participation in them.

In 1785 Place was apprenticed to a leather breeches maker and after four years he set up on his own. The trade was already in decline so life was a perpetual struggle, work was hard to come by and money scarce. But by industry and thrift he and his young wife eked out a frugal living.

However, in 1793, the Breeches Makers' Benefit Society, of which Francis Place was a member, went on strike for better pay. Though not a party to the decision, he was sacked, and by way of response he set about busying himself with the organization of the strike. His careful management of the strike funds enabled the strike to drag on for four months before it collapsed – a fact the bosses were quick to avenge. He found himself a marked man, unable to find work anywhere. He and his young wife

suffered every kind of privation consequent on want of employment and food and fire.

He later reflected:

Persons who have never been in such circum-

27 A view of Charing Cross, London, looking up the Strand, printed in 1811.

stances, can form but faint ideas of the misery even the best and most frugal of workmen sometimes endure.

To counteract his depression and despair, he read. He scrimped and saved to buy books on law, politics, philosophy, history, economics – almost anything that provided food to satisfy his intellectual, sharpened by his physical, hunger.

After some eight months one of his former employers relented and gave him work. The situation eased temporarily, though it remained precarious. Brief periods of work punctuated long spells of unemployment. But Francis Place never wasted his time; he continued his self-education and sought actively to participate in the process of improving the lot of his fellow-workers. He was elected Secretary of his trade society and quickly gained concessions from the employers, through negotiation rather than confrontation, always his preferred course of action.

He joined the Committee of the London Corresponding Society, an organization committed to seeking to achieve parliamentary reform; its members, mostly artisans and small shopkeepers, were at that time largely excluded from the political process.

In 1795 the passing of the "Pitt Acts" and the "Grenville Acts", designed to extend the scope of the Laws against Sedition and Treasonable Assembly, curtailed the Society's activities. However, they continued to meet, though in smaller numbers and with less unity of view. The most radical members became increasingly dominant, and Francis Place, essentially a moderate by temperament and conviction, resigned in 1797. Soon after, in 1798, the remaining members of the Committee were arrested and imprisoned, without trial, for three years, during which time Francis Place organized collections to provide for the needs of their familes.

Disenchanted with politics, Francis Place concentrated on the needs of his growing family (by 1799 he had three young children to feed and clothe).

In 1799 he opened a tailor's shop in the Charing Cross Road, in partnership with a friend and fellow-worker, Richard Wild, who later proved himself untrustworthy and an unscrupulous business-associate. After about a year the partnership was broken up and Francis Place found himself bereft of both business and home, his lodgings having been above the shop.

Bitterly disappointed, frustrated and angry, in April 1801 he set himself up in a new business, with the assistance of a number of genuine friends. Long hours and hard work were rewarded with increasing success.

For the next few years he concentrated on building up his trade and establishing his reputation, though he continued to set aside two to three hours each day for his private reading. A ruminative, reflective man, he later noted in his *Autobiography* the three things that he constantly kept in mind during these years:

28   A portrait of Francis Place (*c.* 1833).

The first, and far the most important, was to get money, and yet to avoid entertaining a mercenary, money-getting spirit; to get money as a means to an end, and not for its own sake. The second was to take care that the contumelious [insolent], treatment I had to endure should not make me a sneaking wretch from principle to those below me. The third was to beware of presumption, that I did not become arrogant.

His interest in politics and social issues remained, but it was not until 1807 that he finally gave way to the urgings of his friends and agreed to play a more active role in seeking to bring about the reforms his conscience told him were essential for the creation of a more just and equitable society. In that year he effectively managed the parliamentary campaign of Sir Francis Burdett, the outspoken reformist candidate at the Westminster election. Against strong competition, Burdett was elected by a majority of 5000 votes. However, though the victory was his, the real architects of this triumph for the cause of reform were Francis Place and his dedicated fellow campaigners who had spent 17 hours a day plotting campaign strategies, canvassing, raising money and encouraging support. Place was deeply proud of the fact that ordinary working men had, by dint of hard work and perseverance defeated the representatives of class privilege and reaction. In his *Autobiography* he boasts with undisguised satisfaction:

We were all of us obscure persons, not one man of note among us, not one in any way known to the Electors generally, as insignificant a set of persons as could well have been collected to undertake so important a public matter as a Westminster Election, against Wealth – and Rank and Name and Influence.

The important lesson it had taught him was that though the political mould could not perhaps be broken, it could be chipped away at successfully if enough men of like mind and principle worked purposefully together to achieve their aims.

For the next 30 years or so Francis Place's library in the back of his shop became a meeting place for those committed to achieving Parliamentary reform. He became a close personal friend of James Mill, the father of the philosopher John Stuart Mill, who, like his son, was a strong advocate of libertarian principles and reform. Place was profoundly influenced by the ideas of Jeremy Bentham, the Utilitarian philosopher and social thinker, although he never became a fully-fledged Benthamite.

For Francis Place the essential aim of all his endeavours was to improve the lives of working people. A committee man by temperament and inclination, he liked to work behind the scenes, leaving the limelight to those better fitted to perform under its searching glare. As Royston Pyke comments in his chapter on Place in *100 Great Nineteenth Century Lives*:

The bitter experiences of his early years had taught him the art of the possible . . . . He knew just how far you could go and get away with. He was a wire-puller of consummate tact and resource. He was a dab hand at writing a letter, framing a manifesto and drawing up a petition.

29 A pro-reformist cartoon showing a radical orator speaking out boldly against the government, whose supporters (on his right) are pictured as ugly, devious or sinister. To his left stand William Cobbett and Sir Francis Burdett, the radicals' candidate for the Westminister Election of 1806.

He loved power, but it was the reality he was concerned with, not the outward show.

From 1807 until 1817 he ran his "gossip shop", advising, cajoling, hectoring and persuading. Then, in 1817 he handed over the running of his business to his eldest son, and, after a period of reflection in the company of Bentham and Mill, set out to give his full time and attention to achieving the political reforms in which he so fervently believed and for which he was to campaign tirelessly for the rest of his life. An equally tireless writer, he died in 1854, leaving to the British Museum over 70 volumes of manuscripts and materials which have ever since proved indispensible to historians of the period.

William Blake (1757-1827)

Virtually unknown outside a small circle of friends and admirers, William Blake received little recognition in his lifetime. Today his stature as a painter, engraver, poet and visionary thinker is universally acknowledged. He was in many ways a solitary man wholly committed to exploring the inner landscape of his own imagination and recording what he saw with "the inward eye". Yet he was also a passionate Radical who counted among his friends such reformers and revolutionaries as William Goodwin, Mary Wollstonecraft and Tom Paine. Unorthodox, anarchic, enigmatic, visionary, Blake's unique genius defies classification: though very much a man of his own times, his voice speaks to, and for, all times.

Blake was born in London on 28 November 1757, the second son of a non-conformist hosier. Acutely sensitive and highly imaginative, from an early age he claimed to have seen angels and biblical characters. At the age of ten he was sent to a drawing academy in the Strand, London, where he studied for four years. During this period he wrote his first verses, later printed in *Poetical Sketches* (1783). Then, from the age of 14 to 20 he was apprenticed to an engraver, James Basire.

In 1778 he enrolled briefly as a student at the newly-founded Royal Academy, but he felt stifled by its dryly academic approach to art, and left to earn his living as an engraver. In 1782 he married the illiterate daughter of a Battersea market-gardener, Catherine Boucher, from whom he was never to be parted until his death in 1827.

Blake opened a small print-seller's shop in 1784 with his brother Robert and a partner. He developed his own method of Illuminated Printing, whereby his poems were first etched

30 William Blake, aged 50. A portrait by Thomas Phillips.

on small copper plates, with pictorial adornments in the margins, then printed and hand-coloured by himself or his wife. The *Songs of Innocence* were produced in 1789, followed in 1790 by a collection of prose epigrams and aphorisms *The Marriage of Heaven and Hell*, and the *Songs of Experience* in 1794.

The *Songs of Innocence* and the *Songs of Experience* complement each other, representing, in Blake's words, the "two contrary states of the human soul".

The *Songs of Innocence*, are mainly poems which celebrate the state of innocence associated by the poet with the experience of childhood, when it is spent in a caring, harmonious, trusting and trustful setting and community. "Innocence" is the child's vision (or the child-like soul's vision) of the human world, uncorrupted by adult experience. The *Songs of Experience* demonstrate how easily this innocence can be corrupted, and joy-in-life replaced by guilt, misery, fears and disillusionment.

Blake associates the world of Innocence with the hospitable, mutually-supportive communities of rural England, and the world of experience with the cities. In the *Songs of Experience*, as Peter Coveney in *The Image of Childhood* observes:

We enter a different world. The pastoral gives place to the urban. Experience lives among the "charter'd" streets of London.

Coveney is here quoting from Blake's poem "London" which expresses most effectively, and powerfully, Blake's sense of moral and human outrage at the corruption of Innocence by the city-bred cancer of depersonalization and inhumanity. His vision is of a living hell, unredeemed by human love, peopled by such pitiful victims as the child prostitute and the chimney-sweep's boy.

I wander thro' each charter'd street,
Near where the charter'd Thames does flow.
And mark in every face I meet
Marks of weakness, marks of woe.

In every cry of every Man,
In every Infant's cry of fear,

31 A chimney-sweep's boy with soot-blackened face. Read the poem "The Chimney Sweeper" from Blake's *Songs of Experience*.

In every voice: in every ban
The mind-forg'd manacles I hear.

How the Chimney-sweeper's cry
Every black'ning Church appalls;
And the hapless Soldier's sigh
Runs in blood down Palace walls.

But most thro' midnight streets I hear
How the youthful Harlot's curse
Blasts the newborn Infant's tear,
And blights with plagues the Marriage hearse.

The suffering of children outraged Blake: he particularly blamed the early days of the Industrial Revolution for allowing society to lose touch with the essential rhythms of human warmth and compassion, replacing them with the cold, harsh, inhuman rhythms of the machine. In such a society "it is eternal winter". In "Holy Thursday", from the *Songs of Experience*, an indignant Blake asks:

Is this a holy thing to see
In a rich and fruitful land,
Babes reduced to misery,
Fed with cold and usurous hand?

Is that trembling cry a song?
Can it be a song of joy?
And so many children poor?
It is a land of poverty.

Blake was profoundly distressed by what he saw in the London of the last decade of the eighteenth century; it was "a terrible desert" inhabited by men, women and children whose poverty was not only physical but spiritual. For this Blake blamed the Church, which he considered to be so preoccupied with preaching and enforcing a restrictive moral code that it failed in its true mission – to bear witness to the great spiritual truths of Christianity. His poem "The Garden of Love" expresses this powerfully:

I went to the Garden of Love,
And saw what I never had seen –
A chapel was built in the midst,
Where I was used to play on the green.

And the gates of this chapel were shut,
And "thou shalt not" writ over the door;
So I turned to the Garden of Love,
That so many sweet flowers bore;

And I saw it was filled with graves,
And tombstones where flowers should be;
And priests in black gowns were walking their
   rounds,
And binding with briars my joys and desires.

Above all else, Blake believed in the God-given potential of man, himself created in God's image.

. . . the worship of God is honouring his gifts
In other men and loving the greatest men best,
                  each according
To his Genius which is the Holy Ghost in Man;
                  there is no other
God than that God who is the intellectual
                  fountain of humanity.

These lines are taken from Blake's last great epic poem "Jerusalem" which he began in 1804 and finally completed, with illustrations, in 1820. Blake had begun to create what he termed his "Prophetic Books" in the late 1780s – and the writing of them was to obsess him for the rest of his life. Between 1789 and 1796 he produced *Tiriel* (1789), *The French Revolution* (1791) *The Visions of the Daughter of Albion* (1793), *America* (1793), *Europe* (1794), *The Book of Urizen* (1794), *The Song of Los* (1795), and the unfinished "Vala of the Four Zoas".

As Jacob Bronowski wrote of them in his introduction to the Penguin Poets book *William Blake*:

The prophetic writings are an immense commonplace book in which Blake wrote night after night much of what came into his head, in an endless commentary on his spiritual and physical life.

They also inspired some of Blake's greatest and most dramatic illustrations, which sadly were only seen by a tiny number of his contemporaries.

Throughout these years, spent living and working in Lambeth, Blake had responded to the political events of the day with typical candour and integrity. A radical by conviction, and an anarchist by temperament, he mistrusted all forms of authority and the law as much as he mistrusted organized religion: "Prisons are built with stones of Law" he declared, and "Brothels with bricks of religion".

His epic poems *The French Revolution* and *America* are poems to the revolutionary spirit, which he believed was born of the Divine energy, and though he was deeply shocked by the horrifying excesses of the Reign of Terror, he remained a staunch supporter of radical reforms until his death. Sadly his radical politics hampered his recognition as a creative artist.

32 Extract from *A Divine Image*, a poem written and engraved by William Blake.

In 1800 his anxious friends persuaded him to leave London; he moved with his wife into a cottage by the sea at Felpham, in Sussex, at the invitation of the country squire and poet, William Hayley, who provided him with a number of commissions.

There he remained for three years, but grew increasingly restless, chafing at Hayley's "genteel ignorance" and attempts to influence him towards producing more conventional work. He determined to return to London, despite his financial loss, but just before he finally left Felpham, Blake found himself in court on trial for sedition after forcibly evicting a drunken soldier from his garden. Fortunately, he was acquitted.

Back in London he settled at 17 South Molton Street, and there began writing and illustrating his two immensely long visionary books *Milton* and *Jerusalem*. He struggled to earn a living from designing and engraving but, though both he and his wife lived frugally, they came at times close to destitution, being rescued only by the good offices of friends. Frequently passed over for lucrative commissions, which went to inferior talents, and, on occasions deceived into producing work for little gain, Blake endured what he felt unable to alter.

In 1809 he made one last attempt to gain wider recognition for his work by mounting a one-man exhibition in his brother's rooms in Soho. It proved a failure, attracting few visitors and exciting little interest.

It was a deeply depressing time for Blake: the few commissions he received came from friends and admirers of his work such as Thomas Butts, John Flaxman and Rev. Joseph Thomas who sought to sustain both the creative dynamism of his genius and his physical well-being. In 1815 Blake's need was such that he accepted a commission from Joseph Wedgwood to draw and engrave examples of his firm's chinaware pottery for his salesmen's pattern-books. However, it was also the year in which he produced his remarkable illustrations to John Milton's masque *Comus*: although commissioned and paid for by Thomas Butts, they are clearly the products of Blake's own visionary imagination, and his lifetime interest in the poet's works (he also illustrated *Paradise Lost*, "L'Allegro" and "Il Penseroso").

Blake continued to decline, dogged by poverty and neglect. However, in 1818 he was introduced to the young painter John Linnell, who not only provided him with valuable commissions at the very time when Thomas Butts's patronage was waning, but also brought his work to the attention of other young painters, such as John Varley and Samuel Palmer. Palmer recognized Blake's genius and also looked to him for guidance and inspiration. Encouraged by their enthusiasm Blake completed, in 1825, what many believe to be his masterpiece, his *Illustrations of the Book of Job*.

He died on 12 August 1827.

SOLDIERS AND SAILORS

In this section we will examine the experiences of the men who fought in the front line during the Napoleonic Wars, whether on land in Wellington's army or at sea in Nelson's navy. What was life like for them? The major events of the wars fought with France between 1793 and 1815 are given in the Date List on pages 62-63.

We have several first-hand accounts of army life during the Napoleonic Wars, and a smaller number of classic accounts of life "below decks" (see list of recommended autobiographical writings on page 62). The autobiographies of John Kincaid, John Shipp, William Richardson and others are so vivid that, when we read their books, we smell the chordite of the cannons, see the heaps of mangled battlefield corpses, hear the pitiful cries of slaves from the stinking prison of the ship's hold.

33 The Duke of York's reforms brought about a new concern for smart appearance and disciplined drilling in the army.

What else do we learn? That when war broke out in 1793 the British army was in a sorry state: most officers were incompetent and most ordinary soldiers were "the scum of the earth" as Wellington himself called them, though he added "it is really wonderful we should have made them the fine fellows they are". Rather, the "fine fellows" they became by the time they marched into France in 1814, not least because Wellington had restored to them their self-respect. The soldiers who fought under Wellington rarely recorded any affection for him, but they respected his judgement. The truth was that Wellington, though a harsh disciplinarian and a stickler for "good form", was an exceptionally brave, astute and resourceful commander of troops in battle. His men trusted him, and when called upon to do so, fought like lions.

Wellington had been able to build upon the army reforms instituted by the Duke of York following the disastrous opening campaign of the war in the Netherlands (1794). These were designed to improve the efficiency of the officers who led and the men who followed. Though he stopped short of abolishing the purchase system (whereby commissions in the army could be bought), he put a stop to officers buying themselves into field rank before they had any experience of active service. He also introduced a system of confidential reports on the competence and efficiency of officers, which was greatly resented but proved remarkably effective. At the same time he saw to it that the ordinary soldier was better dressed, fed, paid, accommodated and, above all, trained.

In 1803 General Sir John Moore developed, at his camp at Shorncliffe, a system of training light infantry which emphasized the need for co-operation and mutual respect rather than coercion. So successful was he that Philip Hammond of the Blues said that Moore's brigade was considered "the finest in respect every sort of danger and deprivation, as Captain Kincaid vividly describes, but survived to perform remarkable feats of arms. Prone to plundering and drunkenness when the opportunity arose, they learned discipline the hard way from Wellington, who never spared the lash and was known to hang serious offenders in order to encourage the others. By the end of the Peninsular campaign they were battle-hardened veterans, a match even for Napoleon's indominatable "Old Guard". Few of them, alas, had the chance to test their mettle against the "Old Guard" at the Battle of Waterloo, since most had been paid off or shipped overseas after Napoleon's abdication.

Wellington's army at the Battle of Waterloo in 1815 was a curiously mixed force: of 67,000 men, only 24,000 were British (the rest were Germans, Dutch and Belgians), and most of them were young and inexperienced. However, on the days of reckoning they proved their worth, in line and in square: standing their ground they broke the final assault of the previously invincible "Old Guard", and won for Wellington a historic victory (albeit assisted by the timely arrival of Marshal Blücher's Prussian army).

After Waterloo the British army's reputation was at its peak and for a time it was even more popular with the nation than Nelson's navy. From the first the British people had

34 Two Privates from the First Guards Regiment.

of discipline that ever was formed in England". The spirit of Moore's innovations spread throughout the army, and though Wellington did not share all Moore's ideas, he welcomed the improvement in training and morale which they inspired.

Wellington's own Peninsular army endured

35 An artist's heroic view of mounted French Cuirassiers charging a British square at the height of the Battle of Waterloo.

known that the navy was the principle guardian of the nation's freedom, and so it proved. By contrast to the army the navy was well prepared for war; when it broke out 55 ships of the line were in fighting trim and ready for action (a brief scare in 1790 had ensured this). During the first decade of the war the British navy was more than a match for its French (and indeed pro-French Dutch and Danish) counterparts. A series of crucial victories at the Battle of the Glorious First of June (1794), St Vincent, Aboukir Bay (The Battle of the Nile), Camperdown (1797), and Copenhagen (1801) paved the way for the greatest maritime victory in the history of the Royal Navy when Nelson's fleet virtually annihilated Napoleon's Mediterranean fleet, at Trafalgar in 1805.

Although the French navy was comparable in strength to the British, it was consistently defeated in battle by the Royal Navy. This was because the Royal Navy had better commanders and officers including Nelson (until his death at Trafalgar), Jervis, Cornwallis, Collingwood, Samuel and Alexander Hood, and the remarkable, if eccentric, Sir Sidney Smith; its ships were better maintained and equipped (with the chronometer, a navigational aid, for example); its seamen were better trained. Most crucially, whereas the French were essentially negative and defensive in their approach to warfare at sea, the British were always looking to attack.

So unless a battle was unavoidable the French preferred to remain in harbour, and the British were happy to keep them there. If the French did venture out they risked a bloody and costly engagement. The Battle of Trafalgar took place only because Napoleon, in a fit of frustrated pique, ordered his fleet to give battle. After Trafalgar he had little enough of a fleet left with which to fight. The Royal Navy consistently thwarted his ambitions and frustrated his enterprises: at the Battle of the Nile at Aboukir Bay in 1798 Nelson's fleet destroyed Napoleon's and cut off his army in Egypt; the Royal Navy's stranglehold on the seas forced him to abandon his cherished plan for invading Britain. Trafalgar was the last straw. In 1814, sitting at the table of the captain of HMS *Bellerophon*, to whom he had surrendered himself, Napoleon said:

If it had not been for you English I would have been Emperor of the East; but wherever there is water to float a ship, we are sure to find you in our way.

What then of the lives of the men responsible – the British seamen? For them life was harsh, often brutal, and frequently highly dangerous. Their food was disgusting and full

36 A cartoon by Rowlandson satirizing the relish with which ships' officers drank their ration of grog.

37 HMS *Victory* breaking the line of French battle ships at the Battle of Trafalgar.

of maggots, their living conditions were cramped and airless, their pay inadequate. Discipline was strict, and flogging for minor offences common. So why did men endure such miseries? Most because they had to: once they were in the navy the only way out was desertion (which was fearfully punished) or death, until the navy chose to dispense with a man's services. Though some sailors were volunteers many were "pressed men", the victims of press-gangs which preyed on seaports the length and breadth of Britain. It seems extraordinary that men treated in this manner should have fought with such bravery and determination when called upon to do so: but they did, time after time, although not always without complaint. In 1797 a serious mutiny broke out at Spithead: the horrified

38 The assembled ship's company watches a sailor being flogged on the "grills".

Lords of the Admiralty at first threatened, then cajoled, and finally compromised: most of the mutineers' demands were met, and order was restored (a later mutiny at the Nore in Kent was suppressed by force, and its leaders hanged). Thereafter the seaman's lot gradually improved, on the lines recommended by such humane officers as Nelson, though it remained an insecure and hazardous existence, as William Richardson so vividly testifies. Nonetheless they did their duty because as G. M. Trevelyan in his *English Social History* notes:

the men before the mast knew that, for all the ill treatment they received, the nation regarded them as its bulwark and its glory; that, at the sight of one of Nelson's men with his tarry pig-tail, the landsman's eye kindled with affection and pride. The country that used them so ill, looked to them confidently to protect her, and they knew it.

Captain John Kincaid (1787-1862)

He was born into a comfortably well-off family in 1787 at Dalheath, near Falkirk in Scotland. After a brief commission as Lieutenant in the North York Militia, he joined the 2nd Battalion Rifle Brigade (then the 95th) at Hythe Battacks in the spring of 1809, as a volunteer. In his autobiography, *Adventures in the Rifle Brigade*, Kincaid implies that this was when his life really began. His first experience of active service was ill-fated; on the expedition to Walcheren in Holland he fell victim to swamp fever and was sent home to recuperate.

In the spring of 1810 he rejoined his battalion which, shortly afterwards, was shipped out to reinforce Wellington's Peninsular army in Portugal. When the battalion was landed at Figuera Bay Kincaid described how they were

welcomed by about a hundred Portuguese women, whose joy was so excessive that they waded up to their armpits through a heavy surf, and insisted on carrying us on shore on their backs.

With characteristically wry humour he adds,

I have never clearly ascertained whether they had been actuated by the purity of love or gold!

Lieutenant Kincaid joined Wellington's forces at a depressing time when they were, effectively, in full retreat before the French forces of General Massena. Spain had been abandoned and Portugal invaded. However, after repulsing a French onslaught at the Battle of Bussaco in September 1810, Wellington's army dug in behind the great defensive lines of Torres Vedras outside Lisbon, and Massena's advance foundered.

The French withdrew to Santarem on 10 November stealing a march on Wellington by "leaving some stuffed straw gentlemen occupying their usual posts". Both sides then settled down to endure the rigours of the Portuguese winter, within rifle-shot of each other.

In March 1811 Massena began a general withdrawal of his army from Santarem and, if Kincaid's account is to be believed, left behind grim reminders of his forces' occupation. In a small country town Kincaid's battalion came upon a sickening sight:

Young women were lying in their houses brutally violated — the streets were strewn with broken furniture, intermixed with the putrid carcasses of murdered peasants, mules and donkeys, and every description of filth that filled the air with pestilential nausea. The few starved male inhabitants who were stalking amid the wreck of their friends and property, looked like so many skeletons who had been permitted to leave their graves for the purpose of taking vengence on their oppressors.

In fact, appalling atrocities were committed by both sides but Kincaid understandably tends to draw attention to the barbarism of his enemies, whilst playing down that of his fellows.

As the French retreated so the British pursued: Marshal Ney, dubbed "the bravest of the brave" by Napoleon, led the French rearguard in a series of bloody actions which bought valuable time for Massena's footsore columns. Kincaid was present at one such skirmish at Ceira, when, for once, Ney was surprised and many of his men were drowned trying to escape from the "furious attack" of the British foot soldiers. Kincaid himself received a musket-ball in the head and was left for dead: fortunately he was taken to a field-hospital and recovered to fight another day.

On 3 April 1811 Kincaid's division took part in the Battle of Sabagul, and were commended for their bravery in Wellington's despatches. They were then marched off to join the forces besieging the French-held fortress of Almeida, and again fought gallantly when, at the Battle of Fuentes De Onoro, a French army sought unsuccessfully to relieve the town. A few days earlier Wellington had returned from consultations to take command of the British forces, and Kincaid expressed the commonly-held view that:

we would rather see his long nose in the fight than the re-inforcement of ten thousand men any day.

In June 1811 Kincaid's division was ordered to march to Estramedura; on route they halted in the village of Soito where some of them dined inside the trunks of enormous chestnut trees.

Kincaid's battalion wintered outside the walls of Cuidad Rodrigo, a French stronghold. There he and his fellow officers enjoyed the local pleasures to the full, proving enthusiastic students of Spanish dances like the bolero and fandango, especially when tutored by the local village girls.

1812 began dramatically with the successful storming of Cuidad Rodrigo by the British and Portuguese forces on 19 January after ten days of hard fighting. Kincaid himself had headed a storming party and he records his thoughts as he lay awake that night:

There is nothing in this life half so enviable as the feelings of a soldier after a victory. Previous to a battle, there is a certain sort of something that pervades the mind, which is not easily defined; it is neither akin to joy nor fear, and, probably, anxiety may be nearer to it than any other word in the dictionary; but when the battle is over, and crowned with victory, he finds himself elevated for a while into the regions of heavenly bliss.

However,

39 Captain Kincaid's regiment, the 95th Rifles, in action at Waterloo.

as the sun began to rise, I began to fall from heroics; and, when he showed his face, I took a look at my own, and found that I was too unclean a spirit to worship, for I was covered with mud and dirt, with the greater part of my dress torn to rags.

For the fighting soldier in Wellington's army, after the intoxication of victory it was always business as usual on the following day; though not before the spoils of victory had been gathered. Kincaid describes how the 5th division marched out of Cuidad Rodrigo:

Some of them were dressed in Frenchmen's coats, some in white breeches and huge jackboats, some with cocked hats and queues [wigs]; most of their swords were fixed on their rifles, and stuck full of hams, tongues and loaves of bread, and not a few were carrying birdcages!

Kincaid next saw action in the bloody assault on the French stronghold of Badajoz on 6 April 1812. For many hours the outcome was uncertain as wave upon wave of British and Portuguese troops stormed forward and were flung back. Kincaid's own regiment suffered terrible losses, many cut down as they attempted acts of "desperate bravery". Finally a breach was made and, after further ferocious hand-to-hand fighting, the castle fell. What then ensued shocked even the battle-hardened Kincaid. In Philip Guedalla's phrase "discipline dissolved in floods of wine": looting was universal, rape and murder common, as the battle-maddened men ran amok. It was three days and nights before order was restored.

Nonetheless, the fall of Badajoz meant that the way was clear for Wellington to march eastwards into Spain; and this he did in June 1812. After marching triumphantly into Salamanca, and clearing the French out of some strongly defended forts outside the town, Kincaid and his regiment marched on into the wine-producing region of the Douro river. There they occupied the town of Rueda, taking full advantage of its local entertainments; the handsome, six-foot tall Johnny Kincaid took his pleasures where he found them, since he knew that each day might be his last.

On 22 July Wellington's forces attacked the army of General Marmont at the Battle of Salamanca after the French had made the mistake of moving across the British army's front, unaware of the danger. It was to prove an important victory for Wellington, who for the loss of some 5000 men inflicted 13,000 casualties on the enemy. Kincaid's division, to his disappointment, "came in for a very slender portion of this day's glory", being held in reserve until the latter stages of the battle.

However, in August, Kincaid's division was in the vanguard when the British army entered the Spanish capital, Madrid, to a tumultuous welcome from its citizens. They "remained there for three months, basking in the sunshine of beauty, harmony and peace ... the most pleasing event of my military life."

This pleasant sojourn came to an end in October when Wellington, threatened by three French armies simultaneously, ordered his remaining troops in Madrid to retreat to Salamanca. This retreat, undertaken in torrential rains which turned the roads into mudbaths, terminated the campaign of 1812.

Kincaid's battalion wintered in the tiny village of Alameida, where they remained until May 1813 when they were once more assembled, for Wellington's renewed offensive against the French. After a long, arduous march across central Spain in the hot summer sunshine they brought to battle the main French army commanded by Napoleon's brother Joseph, who had been proclaimed King of Spain, on 21 June. At the battle of Vittoria the French were routed. "King" Joseph fled the field, leaving behind his army's entire artillery and wagon supplies, and his own personal fortune. Kincaid's division played a notable part in the fighting throughout, were in the thick of the battle, and were in the vanguard in the pursuit of the retreating French. It was a crucial victory: ahead lay the Pyrenees, and France itself.

It took many months for Wellington and his dogged army to fight their way through the wild, rugged, wind-swept scenery of the

Pyrenees, to the French border. The French, commanded by Marshal Soult, fought obstinately but Wellington's men were undeterred: Pamplona and San Sebastian both fell and the road to France was open. On 8 October, Kincaid found himself standing on French soil.

Wellington's army pressed on inexorably, defeating the French at the Battle of Nivelle in November, and at a series of battles around Bayonne in December, which were fiercely contested before the French withdrew.

Kincaid's division had fought hard throughout the campaign, taking part in almost all the major battles. Battle-seasoned but also battle-weary they were delighted when, early in 1814, they found themselves transferred to Saint Jean de Luz, a pretty seaside town where the young ladies "joined in the waltz right merrily", as Kincaid wryly notes, having first "arranged it with their consciences".

In February Wellington resumed his progress eastwards. On the 27th Kincaid's division "marched all day to the tune of a cannonade". It was the Battle of Orthes, from which encounter they were kept in reserve, occupying the town of St Palais instead. Some weeks later they met a strong French contingent occupying a hillside near Tarbes: "after a desperate struggle of a few minutes . . . we drove them from the field with great slaughter." Kincaid proudly records the fitting tribute to his remarkable regiment made by the author of *Twelve Years Military Adventure* who witnessed the assault:

Nothing could exceed the manner in which the 95th set about the business . . . I never saw such skirmishes . . . they could do the work much better and with infinitely less loss than any other of our best light troops. They possessed an individual boldness, a mutual understanding, and a quickness of eye, in taking advantage of the ground which, taken all together, I never saw equalled.

Three weeks later the 95th marched triumphantly into Toulouse after a ferocious assault by the British forces had caused Marshal Soult to withdraw his troops from the city. That same day news came of Napoleon's abdication. The war was over.

Coming to terms with this sudden removal of their *raison d'être* was hard for Kincaid and many of his fellow-soldiers:

We had been born in war, reared in war, and war was our trade; and what soldiers had to do in peace, was a problem yet to be solved amongst us.

As it was they were sent to Castle Sarrazin to await embarkation for England.

Back home, Kincaid returned to Scotland to enjoy some rest and relaxation. It was shortlived. In the spring of 1815 news came to him of Napoleon's escape from Elba, and his return to France. Kincaid's regiment embarked immediately for Holland, and he followed by ship from Leith. From Rotterdam he hurried to join his regiment in Brussels.

A fortnight of inactivity followed while the British and Prussian armies waited for Napoleon to make his move. On 16 June 1815 he struck his first blow, giving Blücher's Prussians what Wellington described as "a damned good hiding!", and forcing their withdrawl from their positions at Ligny. Kincaid's regiment also saw action that day, defending the British position at the crossroads of Quatre Bras, before falling back to a new position near the village of Waterloo.

Next morning Kincaid woke to find himself "drenched with rain", and his horse missing. Fortunately, he recovered his horse, and the weather cleared as the morning advanced. His battalion was ordered to take up position a hundred yards (91.44m) to the rear of La Haye Sainte, to the left of Wellington's centre. When the Battle commenced in earnest Kincaid was in the thick of fierce fighting as the enemy advanced in great numbers on Hougoumont. He and his men were at the centre of:

one continued blaze of musketry . . . the smoke hung so thick about us that, although not more than 80 yards asunder, we could only distinguish our enemy by the flashes of the pieces.

Throughout the afternoon the ferocious fighting continued and by early evening

40 English forces storm the breach at Cuidad Rodrigo. Captain Kincaid himself led a storming party during the assault.

Kincaid, whose horse had been shot dead beneath him, found himself surrounded by the dead and dying. The carnage had been appalling. Walking a little way to each flank he saw "nothing but the mangled remains of men and horses", and reflected

I had never yet heard of a battle in which everybody was killed; but this seemed likely to be an exception, as all were going by turns.

Nonetheless, he also was aware that

however desperate our affairs were, we had still the satisfaction of seeing that theirs were worse.

In fact the tide of battle had already turned against the French: for the first time the advance of the Imperial Guard had been broken, and Napoleon's army was in full retreat.

On the day after the battle Wellington's army commenced its march for Paris. And there Johnny Kincaid ends his narrative.

Little further is known of him except that he received his captain's commission (somewhat tardily) in 1826. Later in 1844, after leaving the army, he was given a place in the Yeomen of The Guard. In 1852 he was knighted, and in 1862 he died.

41 The aftermath of battle. An artist's depiction of the carnage at the Battle of Waterloo.

John Shipp (1784-1834)

John Shipp was brought up with his brother as an orphan in the parish poor-house at Saxmundham in Suffolk, where he was born. His mother had died when he was very young and his father was a soldier "in foreign climes". In his *Memories of the Extraordinary Military Career of John Shipp* he recounts that he was:

thrown on the world's tempestuous ocean, to buffet with the waves of care and to encounter the breakers of want.

In 1793 his elder brother was the victim of a press gang and found himself on board a man-of-war. John Shipp never saw or heard of him again. Left behind in the poor-house he felt friendless and isolated, but he was determined to be a survivor.

The next year brought an incident which was later to change John Shipp's life. He records:

One autumn's morning, in the year 1794, while I was playing marbles . . . the shrill notes of a fife, and the hollow sound of a distant drum, struck on my active ear. I stopped my shot, bagged my marbles, and scampered off to see the soldiers.

It was a recruiting party of the Royal Artillery. The ten-year old John's eye was taken by a figure no bigger than himself:

The pretty little well-dressed fifer was the principal object of my notice. His finery and shrill music were of themselves sufficient attractions to my youthful fancy; but what occupied my thoughts more than either of these was the size of this musical warrior, whose height very little exceeded that of the drum by which he stood.

Then, the recruiting sergeant began his "pitch", looking to stir up the local youths to deeds of daring. His speech was all about:

gentlemen soldiers . . . merry life . . . muskets

42 A recruiting sergeant of the 33rd Regiment drums up recruits outside a hostelry aptly named the "Lord Wellington".

rattling . . . cannons roaring . . . drums beating . . . colours flying . . . regiments charging . . . and shouts of "Victory! Victory!"

And it had the required effect on at least one young inhabitant of Saxmundham:

I adjusted my hat with a knowing air, elevated my beardless chin with as much consequence as I could assume, and, raising myself on tiptoe, to appear as tall as possible, I strutted up to the sergeant, and asked him if he would "take I for a sodger?"

The sergeant, amused by the boy's impudence sent him on his way with a kind word, but from that time onwards Shipp could think of nothing but "soldiering".

Shortly afterwards he was sent to work for a local farmer and although the farmer was a harsh taskmaster, his wife proved a second mother to him and he grew to love and respect her. However, John's life was hard and at times cruel: he was whipped savagely when his master was dissatisfied with his work. He gritted his teeth and endured.

One bitterly cold December day, he heard once more the music of marching soldiers, and dashed from the field where he was working to follow them. Unfortunately, his master followed him, whip in hand. He had scarcely time enough to salute (with the wrong hand) the colonel of the regiment before he was forced to run off at top speed to avoid a public beating. The beating, however, came later and the boy determined to run away and once more try to enlist. He followed the regiment all the way to Beccles, some 16 miles (25km) away, but was again met with a rebuff: the good-natured Colonel told him that he was still too young but gave him some money and sent him back home in the charge of a sergeant, with a note requesting the farmer to show leniency to the boy. The farmer "forgave and forgot" for as long as the sergeant was present, then whipped the boy ferociously.

And so John Shipp's miserable existence continued until, about a year later, his deliverance came in an unexpected way. The government had, by then, come up with a scheme to allow poor-house boys as young as ten years of age to enlist in certain "experimental" regiments of the army – so relieving parishes of a financial burden and swelling the ranks at the same time. A local parish officer, knowing of John Shipp's hopes, brought him the news while he was at work in the fields; he instantly agreed to enlist, and set off for Colchester, where he joined the 22nd Cheshire Regiment of Foot on 17 January 1797.

There he was kitted out in a red jacket, waistcoat, pantaloons and foraging cap, and his hair (or what was left of it by the army barber) was tied back painfully in the fashion of the time, as he ruefully records:

When I was dressed for parade, I could scarcely get my eyelids to perform their office; the skin of my eyes and face was drawn so tight by the plug that was stuck in the back of my head that I could not shut my eyes.

He was put into the regimental band, and, after a short time, made fife-major:

No small office, I assure you. I wore two stripes and a tremendous long sash, which almost touched the ground.

In time his red coat was replaced by a white silver-laced jacket with silver epaulettes, of which he was immensely proud. However, he was constantly in trouble with his peers, who were less than impressed by his swollen-headedness, and his mischievous delight in practical jokes, or "frolics", at their expense, which included:

filling the pipes of my comrades with gunpowder; putting a lighted candle in their hands while asleep, then tickling their noses with a straw; tying their great toes together, then crying out fire; blacking their hands with soot, then tickling their ears and noses, to induce them to scratch themselves and thus to blacken their faces all over; putting lighted paper between their toes while asleep.

He got himself into many "scrapes" and was

caught and severely punished.

When his regiment was embarked for Guernsey a ferocious storm, dramatically described in Shipp's memoirs, almost caused the small sloop to founder. Sea-sick and sodden, looking "like a squeezed lemon or the bag of a Scotch pipe" John Shipp led the fife band through the streets of Fort George. Here once again he was soon in trouble and was compelled to wear his coat turned inside out (whence "turncoat") as a mark of his disgrace.

However, the regiment was not long in Guernsey, and his mark of ignominy was removed when the regiment was shipped to Portsmouth in preparation for embarkation to South Africa.

His ship, the *Surat Castle*, already packed with soldiers (many accompanied by wife and children) was filled to overflowing with a large number of penniless and verminous "scars" (East Indian Sailors), most of whom were disease-ridden. Conditions on board ship were appalling, and the pestilential stench between decks was "beyond the power of description".

The storm-tossed voyage was a terrible experience; an epidemic of scurvy, or "sea-fever", broke out, affecting virtually everyone on board, including John Shipp:

My poor legs were as big as drums; my gums swollen to an enormous size; my tongue too big for my mouth; and all I could eat was raw potatoes and vinegar.

By the time the ship reached The Cape of Good Hope many had perished, and those who landed were weak, debilitated and emaciated. However, decent food and clean air soon put the regiment on its feet again, and they marched off to a small coastal army post, where they were troubled by no worse an enemy than marauding baboons. The regiment's final destination, was the Algoa Bay area further inland where the Kaffirs (native black warriors) had risen against the Dutch settlers and committed many atrocities. For two years John Shipp's regiment battled through impenetrable woods, over tremendous hills and through rivers, constantly harassed by the dart-throwing natives, seeking to keep the peace and restore order. They soon resembled "Falstaff's ragged recruits with whom he swore he would not march through Coventry", as John Shipp ruefully records.

Then, in 1801 the Cape of Good Hope was handed over by the British to the Dutch and John Shipp's regiment was ordered to provide an escort for a family of Dutch settlers over land to Cape Town. The dangers of the journey were offset by the attractions of the Dutchman's pretty daughter Sabina, with whom John Shipp quickly fell in love. When they reached Cape Town he determined to desert from the regiment, which had been ordered to India, rather than be separated

43 A drummer and a fifer of the Guards buy themselves a well-earned drink.

from the girl he loved, even though he knew he faced the direst consequences if caught. And caught he was. He was court-martialled and sentenced to receive 999 lashes, or "50 lashes for every year I was old". Fortunately, thanks to the compassion of his commanding officer, he escaped the punishment, but he never saw the girl again.

Shortly afterwards he was shipped along with his regiment to India. There John Shipp's military career advanced rapidly: within a matter of months he was transferred from the drummer's room and promoted to corporal. Six months later he was advanced to the rank of sergeant, and shortly afterwards, to that of bay-sergeant, a highly responsible and coveted appointment with many perks.

John Shipp remained in India for six years, taking part in many campaigns to suppress revolts and restore order. Promoted to a sergeant in the Grenadiers in 1804 he took part in his first full-scale battle, under the command of Lord Lake, and then, on Christmas Eve he was one of the stormers at the capture of Deig, sustaining a severe head wound for his pains.

In January/February 1805 he led the advance party of the storming column in three of the four brave, but unsuccessful, attacks on the rebel-held stronghold of Bhurtpore. The assaults were all beaten back at terrible cost and Shipp sustained serious injuries but his courage and bravery received its reward: in the next general orders he was commissioned

44 The assault and taking of Seringapatam by British forces under the Command of General Harris (1799).

as an ensign in the 65th Regiment and Lord Lake made him a present of two camels, a horse and a tent.

Some months later Lord Lake appointed him lieutenant in the 76th Regiment, with which he remained until 1807 when the regiment was recalled to England.

Unfortunately, John Shipp found himself poorly equipped to cope with civilian life back in England: he was soon in serious debt and forced to sell his commission. After some six months he found himself penniless, homeless and friendless.

He determined to re-enlist and begin again from the bottom of the military ladder. He joined the 24th Light Dragoons in Maidstone, and was soon promoted to the rank of sergeant. On 8 January 1808 he sailed once more for India to join the regiment. There once again he set about creating a reputation for bravery, reliability and soldierly conduct. By 1813 he was Regimental Sergeant-Major Shipp, and in 1815 he was appointed to ensign in the 87th Regiment of Foot. Thus he had twice risen from the ranks to win a commission before he was much more than 30 years old – a remarkable, possibly unique achievement.

He remained in India until 1825, taking an active part in many battles, sieges and skirmishes. Sadly his military career ended in

1825 under a cloud, following his open criticism of superior officers. He spent the last 11 years of his life in Liverpool, first as Superintendent of The Night Watch, then, as Master of the Workhouse. He died on 27 February 1834.

Sir Sidney Smith (1764-1840)

Sidney Smith, later Admiral Sir Sidney Smith, had a distinguished career as a Royal Navy commander and played a vital role in many confrontations during the Napoleonic Wars. He was one of a highly respected military family. At the age of 13, having chosen the Navy as a career, he joined a storeship bound for North America, as a midshipman.

He saw action in a number of engagements with the French over the next few years on board a variety of ships. Then, in October 1782, he was promoted to post-captain of the *Alcmene*. Shortly afterwards hostilities with France ceased and he was offered the command of a guardship. He turned it down and, instead, set off on a tour of the Continent to find out as much as he could about those European nations with whom Britain might one day be at war, or to whom she might be allied.

He went first to France, "the old enemy", renewing his "acquaintance" with many French naval officers against whom he had earlier fought: he was even taken to see the new works at the naval base of Cherbourg.

In 1787, he left France for Gibralter, fluent in the French language and something of an expert on France's maritime defences. From there he travelled through the lands of the Sultan of Morocco, then, on hearing that a war between Sweden and Russia was imminent, he went to Sweden. There King Gustavus IV offered him the command of a "light Squadron", but he could accept only with the permission of the British Admiralty. When this was not granted he returned to Sweden and offered his services to King Gustavus as a volunteer. From then on he acted as the King's aide-de-camp and naval adviser, taking an active part in a number of hard-fought engagements with the Russians. On the declaration of peace in 1791, he was knighted at sea by the grateful monarch for his services to the Swedish nation. On his return to England George III recognized his award and invested him on 19 May 1792.

Later that year the British Foreign Office, as impressed by his independence and resourcefulness as the Lords of the Admiralty were disturbed by his impetuosity, funded Smith on a journey to Turkey, to observe the effects of the war which had broken out between Turkey and Russia. This mission was, however, cut short when war once again

45 A portrait of Sir Sidney Smityh in action at the Siege of Acre.

broke out between Great Britain and Revolutionary France.

He came home through Smyrna and there, as he recorded in a letter:

observed a number of British seamen prowling about the streets, and, acquainting them of the war, found they were willing to enter with me in service.

Together they sailed to join the British fleet at Toulon in a small vessel bought by Sir Sidney from a surprised local. Arriving at Toulon they found a confused situation: the international pro-Royalist force which had been hastily gathered by Lord Hood was about to be overrun by the attacking Revolutionary forces, who were at the town's gates within days. Mass panic ensued and large numbers of pro-Royalists, fearing a massacre, clamoured to be evacuated by sea. Lord Hood did his best to take off as many as he could, but the situation became critical when the attackers broke through the town's outer defences. Sir Sidney and his men assisted in the evacuation and then volunteered to lead a hand-picked force to set fire to as many as possible of the French ships which lay in the harbour, to prevent them falling into enemy hands. With the Revolutionary soldiers and the town's dockyard workers swarming everywhere and butchering indiscriminately, Sir Sidney and his men sailed into the harbour and calmly set light to more than 20 French vessels, before sailing out with decks crammed with Royalist refugees.

Sir Sidney's remarkable achievement was acknowledged by Lord Hood who gave him the honour of carrying the despatches to London, which he did with intense pride. Unfortunately, his pride was seen by many as vanity and conceit: something of an actor by temperament he loved to impress an audience with his tales of daring deeds. This did not go down well with his naval colleagues. Horatio Nelson, in particular, found him insufferably cocksure despite the efforts of the new First Lord of the Admiralty, Lord George Spencer, to present Sir Sidney in a favourable light.

Spencer, though aware of Sir Sidney's weakness, recognized his strengths, and was determined to make good use of them. In 1798 he appointed him Captain of the *Tigre*, a fine two-decker recently captured from the French. In addition Sir Sidney received a Foreign Office commission appointing him joint plenipotentiary, with his brother Spencer Smith, to the court of the Ottoman Emperor at Constantinople, with whom the British government was keen to establish an alliance.

These dual responsibilities afforded Sir Sidney the ideal opportunity to cause mischief by playing off his naval mission against his Foreign Office commission and vice versa whenever it suited him to do so. He irritated almost everybody, especially Nelson, through whose area of command he passed and to whom he sent a number of jaunty but misconceived letters. Letters of complaint about Sir Sidney soon piled up on the First Lord's desk, but he took no action. His confidence in Sir Sidney's ability as a persuasive negotiator was rewarded in January 1799 when a Treaty was signed with the Ottoman Emperor.

After his diplomatic success Sir Sidney returned to his naval duties, directing the blockade of Alexandria. Inland Napoleon, threatened by the pro-Turkish Syrians, set off on a punitive campaign, capturing a string of important towns, including Jaffa. Only Acre stood between him and a clear march to attack Constantinople and crush the Turks. Sir Sidney, recognizing this, was determined to thwart Napoleon's plans; on his own initiative he sent on ahead the brilliant young French emigré military engineer, Phelypeaux, to strengthen the neglected fortifications at Acre. Shortly afterwards he came upon Napoleon's advance guard near Mount Carmel: after scattering them with grapeshot he captured a series of accompanying gunboats which were laden with heavy siege artillery. Arriving at Acre he triumphantly mounted the captured guns on the town walls – pointing them directly at their previous owners.

With the cooperation of Djezzar Pasha, the Governor of Syria, Sir Sidney set about organizing the town's defence, and instilling resolution into its defenders (some 3000 in all, comprising the Turkish garrison and a number of British marines). Over the next few months the French tried every tactic they knew, from costly frontal assaults to siege-mining, but the defences held.

By May Napoleon's patience had run out; hearing of the approach of a Turkish fleet carrying reinforcements, he threw his entire force into a grand frontal assault on the town's defences. The French advanced with reckless courage and breached the town's outer fortifications, despite heroic resistance. They seemed to have victory within their grasp when Sir Sidney led a contingent of British sailors and marines, armed with pikes and cutlasses, at the charge, into the mouth of the breach where the fiercest hand-to-hand fighting was taking place. The French foundered. In the meantime the Turkish reinforcements had arrived from Rhodes and, as they poured into the battle, the tide turned in favour of the defenders. The French retreated in considerable disarray and later, by night, withdrew along the road to Haifa.

Napoleon was furious; it was the first time he had ever suffered a reversal as a commander in a land battle, and he chiefly blamed the young British captain who had undertaken the town's defence on his own initiative. Sir Sidney, for his part, contented himself with a visit to the Cave of the Annunciation in Nazareth, where he gave thanks for his victory.

The news of Sir Sidney's exploits at Acre soon spread far and wide; he became a living legend, his name a byword for heroism and wise council. He took full advantage of this to create and sustain friendships between Britain and the many nations of the Levant.

Meanwhile, Napoleon had defeated a Turkish army at Aboukir Bay, thus salvaging some personal pride, and had sailed for France with a group of his senior officers, leaving the Egyptian Army under the command of General Kleber, to fend for itself.

Sir Sidney was convinced that Kleber should be encouraged, by favourable terms, to sign a peace treaty and ship his army back home to France – thus putting an end to French ambitions in the Levant. So he went ahead and organized a meeting between Kleber and the Grand Vizier; a treaty was signed and Kleber set about honouring its terms by vacating a number of French strongholds.

However, in the meantime, the British government, bowing to pressure from her allies, had decided that the French army might only leave Egypt as unarmed prisoners of war. Sir Sidney was placed in the humiliating position of having to inform Kleber of the British government's new directive. Kleber indignantly re-occupied the

46 Sir Sidney Smith leads a contingent of British sailors and marines into the thick of the hand-to-hand fighting at the critical moment during the siege of Acre, 1799.

strongholds, enraged by what he saw as British treachery.

Sir Sidney felt that he had been "stabbed in the back" by a British government which, by hastily accusing him of "exceeding his powers" sought to excuse its conduct; he also felt certain that a grave mistake had been made.

He was soon proved right. In January 1800 Kleber's troops routed the army of the Grand Vizier at Heliopolis in Egypt, and the British government was forced to ship out an army of 16,000 men under General Abercromby to stablize the situation. When a treaty was finally signed with the French the terms were substantially the same as those of the original treaty. In the meantime many British lives had been lost in achieving a successful outcome to the campaign, including that of General Abercromby. Sir Sidney, for his part, had given his advice when asked, and taken part in a number of bloody engagements with the French; he had also succeeded in having a blazing quarrel with the new British Army Commander, Sir John Hutchinson.

Admiral Keith packed him off back to England with the despatches recording the British "success". He set sail on board the *El Carmen* and, after a number of adventures, landed in Portsmouth on 9 November dressed, as the correspondent of the *Times* reports with a mixture of admiration and astonishment:

in Turkish dress, turban, robe, shawl, and girdle round his waist, with a brace of pistols.

His sole concession to convention was to shave off "a large pair of moustachios" which he had proudly sported in the Levant.

Although in official circles he had frequently been shabbily treated, to the nation at large he was The Hero of Acre; this was also acknowledged by George III, who granted him additional armorial bearings in reward for his gallantry. In London society he was lionized by the ladies, many of whom wore plumed turbans; Egypt was all the rage, and so was Sir Sidney, who hugely enjoyed the fuss and attention.

The Freemen of Rochester sought his candidacy for the borough's Parliamentary seat, and in a letter of acceptance he states his position with typical candour:

My political creed is the English constitution, my party, the nation. Highly as I prize the honour of becoming your representative, I will not purchase that, or any other distinction, by renouncing an atom of my independence.

No one doubted it. He was returned to Parliament with a large majority.

He took his seat in November 1802, some months after the Treaty of Amiens had brought a temporary halt to the war. In the spring of 1803 hostilities were renewed and Sir Sidney was appointed to the *Antelope*, as commodore of a squadron detailed to patrol the Dutch coast. Soon bored with this he asked to be relieved and spent the next 18

47 The fashion for Turkish dress which followed the reporting of Sir Sidney Smith's exploits can be seen in the turban-style hats worn by these society ladies.

months working on some ideas he had for the building of troop-carrying catamarans intended for use in a projected assault on Boulogne, which, in the event, never took place.

Then in November 1805 he was promoted to the rank of rear-admiral, and sent to the Mediterranean to lead a detached command off the coast of Naples. On board his flagship *Pompee* he sailed north to Sicily and supplied the embattled garrison of Gaeta with stores and ammunition, then went off to capture Capri, before returning to Sicily. There he set about arming and training local guerrilla fighters, to the annoyance of the senior British Army officers, who were already outraged by his habit of issuing proclamations under the title of "Commander in Chief on behalf of the King of Naples". Sir John Moore, in particular, took offence at Sir Sidney's flamboyant and high-handed ways. Colonel Bunbury, Moore's Chief of Staff, wrote of him in his *Narrative of Some Passages in the Great War With France*:

He was an enthusiast, always panting for distinction, restlessly active, but desultory in his views, extravagantly vain, daring, quick-sighted, and fertile in those resources which befit a partisan leader; but he possessed no great depth of judgement, nor any fixitive of purpose save that of persuading mankind, as he was fully persuaded himself, that Sidney Smith was the most brilliant of chevaliers.

After a brief expedition to the Dardanelles, he found himself under orders to sail for Lisbon, where he was to effect the safe conduct of the Prince Regent of Portugal and his family across the Atlantic to Brazil, along with the entire Portuguese fleet, which would otherwise have fallen into French hands. He succeeded in his mission and stayed with the Portuguese Royal family in Rio, acting as their naval and diplomatic adviser until he fell foul of the British Ambassador to the exiled Court, Lord Strangford, and was recalled to England.

There he once again cut a dashing figure in society, and wooed and wed Caroline Hearn in October 1810, shortly after being promoted to the rank of vice-admiral. He suspected his days of active service might be over, but in July 1812 he was appointed second-in-command of the Mediterranean Fleet then blockading Toulon. It proved to be a dull affair but he passed the time setting up a ship-board printing press and organizing amateur theatricals. His diplomatic skills were used to renew his country's somewhat frayed ties of friendship with King Victor Emmanuel of Sardinia, who graciously accepted an invitation to dine on board Sir Sidney's flagship.

In April 1814 Napoleon abdicated and the hostilities ended. Sir Sidney hurried home, but soon after set off, accompanied by his wife and her two pretty daughters from a previous marriage, to attend the Congress of Vienna. His purpose was twofold: to plead the cause of his exiled friend King Gustavus IV of Sweden, and also to plead for the establishment of an international force committed to enforcing the release of Christian prisoners held in appalling conditions by the corsairs of the Barbary Coast in North Africa. King Gustavus found few friends, but, as a result of a great dinner thrown by Sir Sidney, a huge sum of money was raised to fund The Knights Liberators of The Slaves in Africa, an association of which he was elected president.

However, before much could be done news came of Napoleon's escape from Elba and his return to France. Sir Sidney, determined to play some role, however small, in the great battle against his old enemy which he knew must follow, set off for Brussels with his family.

On the day of the battle of Waterloo he rode out to the battle field and, in his own words,

I stemmed the torrent of the disabled and giversin the best way I could, was now and then jammed among the broken wagons by a drove of disarmed Napoleonist janissaries, and finally reached the Duke of Wellington's person and rode with him from St Jean to Waterloo . . . . I had the heart-felt gratification of being the first Englishman that was not in the battle who shook hands with him before he got off his horse . . . .

This was a remarkable meeting between two men who had done so much to thwart Napoleon's ambitions over the years.

Sir Sidney accompanied the army to Paris where he was invested by the Duke with the Order of The Bath, in the splendid setting of the Palais Bourbon.

Now 50 years old, Sir Sidney chose Paris for his future home: from there he conducted a huge correspondence related to his anti-slavery campaign. He became a great favourite in Paris society, constantly visited by France's most distinguished men, and befriended by King Louis.

In 1821 he was promoted to the rank of full admiral. In 1826 his wife died, a blow from which he never fully recovered. In 1838 he received the Grand Cross of The Bath from Queen Victoria. He died in Paris in 1840.

William Richardson (1768-1865)

Born in South Shields, Co. Durham, in 1768, the son of a ship's captain, William Richardson, the author of *A Mariner of England*, was destined from the cradle to "go to sea". But his experiences were often far from happy, and his comments show the misery of being a victim of the press gangs. He was sent to study navigation under an incompetent "dram-drinking" old teacher in South Shields. His father took him along on a number of his short voyages to "get his sea-legs", and, though he suffered initially from sea-sickness, he was determined to become a seaman.

In January 1781 he was bound apprentice for seven years to the master of the *Forester*, on which ship he served for six years, initially as cabin-boy, then as a deck-hand, and finally as second mate.

In 1788 in Philadelphia Richardson jumped ship, intending to take his chance on an American vessel, but his captain had him incarcerated in a local jail until the *Forester* set sail for England. Richardson obstinately (as he acknowledges) refused to remain in his captain's service, and left with a paltry 15 shillings in his pocket.

He spent a wretched time unable to find employment before his uncle offered him a place on his sailing ship the *Mosely*. He spent 1789 shipping coals from South Shields to

48 African slaves being fettered before being forced into the stinking confinement of the ship's hold.

London, as he had done as an apprentice.

Early in 1790 he left the *Mosely* to join the crew of the *Spy*, a slaver bound for Guinea, as fourth mate, narrowly avoiding being pressganged into the King's service. They reached Guinea safely, and remained there for some weeks while the ship was gradually filled with slaves bought from the local ruler, King Pepple.

Then, with holds crammed with slaves, they made their way to Montego Bay, Jamaica, to sell their human cargo. Richardson, an essentially humane man, found his captain's cruelty and greed sickening, and he did what little he could to alleviate the slaves' sufferings.

Two days after his return to England, where he was greeted by news of his father's death, he was taken by a press-gang. He was dispirited, but refused to be disheartened by his ill luck, as he writes:

I was young and had the world before me, did not fret much and was willing to go to any part of the world.

Later he viewed the practice differently:

see a poor sailor arrived from a long voyage, exulting in the pleasure of soon being among his dearest friends and relations . . . when a press gang seizes him like a felon, drags him away and puts him into the tender's hold, and from

49 The callous brutality of the press gang, and its effect upon the victim's wife and children, is vividly depicted in this drawing by Rowlandson.

thence he is sent on board a man-of-war, perhaps ready to sail to some foreign station, without seeing either his wife, friends or relations; if he complains he is likely to be seized up and flogged with a cat . . . and if he deserts he is flogged round the fleet nearly to death. Surely they had better shoot a man at once: it would be greater lenity!

Along with a number of his old shipmates, he was sent on board the 98-gun *London*, a far larger ship than any he had been on board before.

Richardson found naval discipline harsh and arbitrary, especially the "starting" (or whipping with rattans, or canes) regularly practised by the boatswain's mates, but he was hardy and not given to self-pity. He endured the privations, and enjoyed the company of his fellows.

After only three months, however, the fleet was paid off, and he was given his freedom. For a time he lived from his savings, but necessity drove him back to sea, and he reluctantly joined the crew of another slaver, which was wrecked trying to enter Ostend harbour to shelter from a fierce storm. Richardson transferred to the *Prince of Kauritz*, a trading ship which sailed for India on 1 June 1791.

Upon reaching Calcutta, Richardson and a dozen other British seamen left the ship rather than sail under a captain they considered "a proud haughty tyrant". Calcutta fascinated Richardson with its extraordinary architecture, atmosphere and customs but he was soon back at sea. After narrowly avoiding death in another shipwreck he returned to his old lodgings in Calcutta, where,

As I was sitting near the door, with it open, and smoking a cheroot [cigar] while brooding over my hard fate, a guard of soldiers came along, and the sergeant seeing me, said that I was to go along with him.

The sergeant had been ordered to "take" every English seaman he could find for service in His Majesty's Navy. Richardson could scarcely believe his ill fortune:

Shipwreck and the loss of all our clothes is distressing enough, but to be pressed into the bargain is really shocking . . . .

An attempted escape proving unsuccessful, he found himself on board the 48-gun frigate, the *Minerva*. He reflected ruefully on his years as a merchant seaman:

Thus ended my services of near thirteen years in the merchant's employ, a period of poverty, hardships, danger and disappointment such as few, I believe, have experienced.

His prospects in the Royal Navy looked bleak enough:

I was stationed to do my duty in the maintop: all my clothes were on my back, and with an old silver watch and one rupee, which constituted my all, I had now, as it were, the world to begin again . . . .

Richardson soon readjusted to the life of a "blue-jacket", and to his surprise he found more to praise than criticize. The ship was well-officered, though the captain was inexperienced: discipline was strict but fair and the men knew where they stood.

While on board the *Minerva* Richardson and his fellows were taught how to handle the musket; their initial incompetence amused him greatly:

Nothing could be more diverting than to see the blunders we made at the first beginnings . . . some put their muskets on the wrong shoulder, some let the butt fall on their neighbour's toes, some could not stand with their backs straight up, and were threatened with a cross-bar lashed to it, and some had their shoulders chalked by the captain, that they might know the right from left . . . .

Richardson served on the *Minerva* for some nine months, revisiting India, from where he returned to England with painful scurvy in May 1794. He was immediately drafted on board the frigate *Prompte*.

However, good provisions, warm clothing and promotion to captain of the maintop

50 Life on board ship was frequently enlivened for the seamen by the presence of their women (not necessarily their wives).

reconciled him to his new situation. In the spring of 1795, a new captain was appointed who brought several of his followers with him. Amongst them, to William's delight was his brother, James Richardson, whom he had not seen for six years, and from whom he learned that all his four brothers were now in the Royal Navy.

Shortly afterwards the *Prompte* put in at Richardson's home port, which he found "gloomy and sad on account of nearly all the young men being pressed and taken away".

After two unsuccessful attempts, thwarted by fierce storms, the *Prompte* finally set sail for the West Indies as part of a small fleet bound for St Lucia, which, soon after her arrival surrendered to the British forces in May 1796.

She returned to Spithead in the summer of 1797, shortly after the Nore mutiny had been quelled, and docked in Portsmouth harbour for repairs. On 23 July William Richardson married Sarah Thompson, the daughter of a Portsea master stone-mason.

Three weeks later he was back at sea returning to the Caribbean for a term of duty which lasted two eventful years, during which time the *Prompte* was frequently involved in bloody encounters with local privateers and French and Spanish ships, and on one occasion was almost sunk by a devastating hurricane off Bermuda.

Returning to England in 1799 Richardson, now a gunner, was appointed to the "Regulars", and so left the "happy *Prompte*". However, before he saw any action on his new ship, he was transferred to the *Tromp* and set sail for Martinique, this time accompanied by his wife, who almost died of fever on the voyage.

The *Tromp* remained in Martinique for two years, being used, to Richardson's disgust, as a prison-ship, before being ordered home in 1802.

During the suspension of hostilities occasioned by the Peace of Amiens Richardson bought a house for his wife, and settled down to enjoy a peaceful spell of home comforts. But his peace proved as shortlived as the Peace of Amiens: in March 1803 hostilities with France were renewed. A general "press" broke out all over England, and Richardson soon found himself back on board the *Tromp*.

In April 1805 he was transferred at his own request, after difficulties with the captain, to the *Caesar* at Plymouth. Within months he saw action in an engagement with some French ships off Brest: a brutal and bloody affair, it was the first time he ever saw "human blood run out of the scuppers". Then in October the *Caesar*, captained by the daring "Mad Dick" Strachan, spearheaded a series of dramatic manoeuvres which led to the capture of an entire squadron of French front-line ships.

During the next two years, Richardson saw service on the *Caesar* in the West Indies, and off the French west coast, before returning to England in October 1808.

In 1809 the *Caesar*, now Rear-Admiral Stapford's flagship, joined the Channel fleet and took part in a number of engagements with the French. In April she participated in the "firing" of the French fleet in Aix harbour; Richardson himself was responsible for fitting-up one of the fire-ships used in the attack.

In July the *Caesar* was used to transport British troops to the Low Countries on the Walcheren Expedition; and later to evacuate those who remained after the failure of the enterprise.

In March 1810 the *Caesar* proceeded to Lisbon, a city whose architectural splendour greatly impressed Richardson, and then returned to England, after an absence of 14 months. She never again put to sea, "being completely worn out". Most of the crew were transferred, but Richardson remained for six idle months, the *Caesar* having been fitted up as a military store-ship.

After two further transfers he was discharged in 1819, and left the King's service with little regret, believing he had been "neglected in promotion". He had been at sea for 39 years.

Richardson lived to the age of 97, and died in Portsmouth in 1865.

Books For Further Reading

General Background
Asa Briggs, *The Age of Improvement*, History of England, vol. 8 (Longman, Green and Co., 1959)
J. Clarke, *The Price of Progress: Cobbett's England 1780-1835* (Hart-Davis, MacGibbon, 1977)
E.J. Evans, *The Forging of the Modern State: Early Industrial Britain 1783-1870* (Longman, 1983)
J.H. Plumb, *The First Four Georges* (Batsford, 1956)

Social histories
B. Inglis, *Poverty and the Industrial Revolution* (Hodder and Stoughton, 1971)
D.A. Low, *That Sunny Dome* (Dent, 1977)
S. Margetson, *Regency London* (Cassell, 1971)
J.B. Priestley, *The Prince of Pleasure and his Regency* (Heinemann, 1969)
E.P. Thompson, *The Making of the English Working Class* (Gollancz, 1980)
G.M. Trevelyan, *English Social History* (Longman, 1978), chapters XV-XVI
R.J. White, *Life in Regency England* (Batsford, 1963)

Contemporary accounts
T. Creevey, *The Creevey Papers*, ed J. Gore (Folio Society, 1970)
L.A. Marchand, ed., *Lord Byron: Selected Letters and Journals* (John Murray, 1982)

Histories of the Napoleonic Wars
N. Harris, *Napoleon* (Batsford, 1988)
A. Brett-James, *Life in Wellington's Army* (George Allen and Unwin, 1979)
I. Fletcher, *In Hell before Daylight* (Baton Press, 1984) (the storming of Badajoz)
M. Glover, *The Napoleonic Wars: An Illustrated History 1792-1815* (Batsford, 1979)
M. Glover, *Warfare in the Age of Bonaparte* (Cassell, 1980)
J.C. Herold, *The Battle of Waterloo* (Cassell, 1967)
D. Howarth, *Trafalgar: The Nelson Touch* (Fontana, 1971)
D. Howarth, *Waterloo: A Near Run Thing* (Fontana, 1972)
L. Kennedy, *Nelson and his Captains* (Collins, 1975)
P. Padfield, *Nelson's War* (Hart-Davis MacGibbon, 1976)
R. Parkinson, *The Peninsular War* (Hart-Davis MacGibbon, 1973)
J. Read, *War in the Peninsula* (Faber and Faber, 1977)

Individual biography
The Prince Regent
C. Hibbert, *George IV* (Penguin, 1976)
A. Palmer, *The Life and Times of George IV* (Cardinal, 1975)
J.B. Priestley, The Prince of Pleasure and His Regency (Heinemann, 1969)
J. Richardson, *George IV: A Portrait* (Sidgwick and Jackson, 1966)

Beau Brummell
H. Cole, *Beau Brummell* (Granada, 1977)
E. Moers, *The Dandy: Brummel to Beerbohm* (Secker and Warburg, 1960)

Jane Austen
R.W. Chapman, ed., *Jane Austen's Letters* (O.U.P., 1955)
J.A. Hodge, *The Double Life of Jane Austen* (Hodder and Stoughton, 1972)
M. Laski, *Jane Austen and her World* (Thames and Hudson, 1969)

William Cobbett
D. Green, *Great Cobbett: The Noblest Agitator* (Hodder and Stoughton, 1983)
J. Sambrook, *William Cobbett* (Routledge and Kegan Paul, 1973)

Francis Place
M. Thrale, ed., *The Autobiography of Francis Place* (C.U.P., 1972)

William Blake
J. Bronowski, *A Man Without a Mask* (Secker and Warburg, 1944)
J. Lindsay, *William Blake* (Constable)
R. Lister, *William Blake* (Bell)

Sir Sidney Smith
P. Shankland, *Beware of Heroes: Admiral Sir*

Sidney Smith's War against Napoleon (Kimber, 1975)

First-hand accounts of life in Wellington's army (1793-1815)
E. Costello, *The Peninsular and Waterloo Campaigns*, ed. A. Brett-Janes (Longman, 1967)
E. Cotton, *A Voice from Waterloo* (EP, 1974) (facsimile of 1849 edition)
M. Glover, ed., *A Gentleman Volunteer: The Letters of George Hennell from the Peninsular War 1823-1813* (Heinemann, 1979)
J. Green, *A Soldier's Life* (EP, 1973)
C. Hibbert, ed., *A Soldier of the Seventy First* (Cooper, 1969)
C. Hibbert, ed., *The Recollections of Rifleman Harris* (Cooper, 1970)
C. Hibbert, ed., *The Wheatley Diary* (Longman, 1964)
General Mercer, *Journal of the Waterloo Campaign* (Greenhill, 1985)

D.S. Richards, *The Peninsula Veterans* (MacDonald and James, 1975 (based on eye-witness accounts)
J. Shipp, *Memories of the Extraordinary Military Career of John Shipp* (Chatto and Windus, 1969) (first published 1829)
J. Kincaid, *Adventure in the Rifle Brigade* (Drew, 1981) (first published 1830)

First-hand accounts of life in Nelson's Navy (1793-1815)
H.W.F. Baynham, *From the Lower Deck: The Old Navy* (Hutchinson, 1969) (with chapters on individual seamen)
J. Hewitt, *Eye-Witness to Nelson's Battles* (Osprey, 1972)
E. Hughes, ed., *The Private Correspondence of Lord Collingwood* (Navy Records Society, 1957)
W. Richardson, *A Mariner of England* (Conway Maritime Press, 1970)
H.G. Thursfield, ed., *Five Naval Journals, 1789-1817* (Navy Records Society, 1951)

DATE LIST

1793
21 January	Louis XVI of France executed.
1 February	France declares war on Britain and Holland.
7 March	First Coalition formed in France.
19 December	Fall of Toulon.
22 December	Napoleon Bonaparte promoted to General of French army.

1794
May	William Pitt suspends Habeas Corpus.
1 June	Battle of The Glorious First of June. British Naval victory.
July-August	French victories in Belgium and on the Rhine.
28 July	Robespierre executed. End of The Reign of Terror.

1795
June-October	Royalist risings in Brittany.
Autumn	Bad harvests lead to food riots in England.
3 November	The Directory installed as government of France.
	Speenhamland Act (Poor Law).

1796
2 March	Napoleon Bonaparte appointed Commander of Army of Italy.
10 May	Battle of Lodi, Napoleon victorious.
19 August	Spain signs treaty with France.
8 October	Spain declares war on Britain.
21-27 December	French land troops in Bantry Bay.
December	Peace negotiations between Britain and France fail.

1797
14 February	Battle of Cape St Vincent. British naval victory.
22-24 February	French troops attempt landing on Welsh Coast.
16 April-5 May	Spithead Mutiny.
12 May-13 June	Mutiny of the British fleet at the Nore, Kent.
11 October	Battle of Camperdown. British naval victory.
17 October	Treaty of Campo Formio between Austria and France.

1798
21 July	Napoleon defeats Mameluke Turks at Battle of the Pyramids.
1 August	Nelson destroys French fleet at Battle of the Nile in Aboukir Bay.
23 August	French troops land in north-west Ireland.
29 December	Second Coalition formed in France.

1799
9 January	Income Tax introduced by William Pitt to help finance the war.
March-May	Siege of Acre.
12 July	"Combination Acts" passed.
24 July	Napoleon wins second Battle of Aboukir Bay.
August	British expedition to Holland.
18 October	British troops leave Holland.
14 December	Napoleon Bonaparte becomes First Consul.

1800
28 March	Act of Union between England and Ireland.
14 June	Napoleon defeats Austrians at Marengo.
5 September	Britain captures Malta.
	Robert Owen opens "model" factory in New Lanark, Scotland.

1801
15 January	Austria makes peace with France.
14 March	Pitt resigns as Prime Minister.
2 April	Battle of Copenhagen. Nelson defeats Danish fleet.

1802
26 January	Napoleon becomes President of Italian Republic.
25 March	Peace of Amiens, between Britain and France.

1803
18 May	Britain declares war on France.
23 September	Battle of Assaye.
	Napoleon prepares for invasion of England.

1804
10 May	Pitt returns as Prime Minister of Britain.
18 May	Napoleon proclaimed Emperor of France.
24 May	Alliance between France and Russia (broken off 3 months later).

1805
26 March	Napoleon crowns himself King of Italy.
11 April	Alliance between Britain and Russia.
9 August	Third Coalition formed.
21 October	Nelson defeats Franco-Spanish fleet at Trafalgar, but dies in action.
	Napoleon abandons plan to invade England.
2 December	Battle of Austerlitz. Napoleon shatters Third Coalition.
15-27 December	Russia and Austria make peace with France.

1806
23 January	Death of William Pitt the younger.
15 February	Prussia signs treaty with France.
16 May	British blockade French ports.
8 October	Prussia declares war on France.
14 October	Prussians defeated at Jena.
27 October	Napoleon enters Berlin.
21 November	Napoleon's Berlin Decrees (also known as the Continental System) close continental ports against English ships.

1807
8 February	Napoleon defeats Russians at Battle of Eylau.
14 June	Russians again defeated, at Friedland.
7-9 July	Treaty of Tilsit between Russia, Prussia and France.
	Britain fights on alone.
11 & 25 November	Britain declares blockage of all French ports and ships.
December	French invade Spain.

1808
6 June	Joseph Bonaparte proclaimed King of Spain.
1 August	Sir Arthur Wellesley lands English troops in Portugal. Beginning of Peninsular campaign.
5 November	Napoleon takes command of French forces in Spain.
2 December	Napoleon captures Madrid.
24 December	Sir John Moore begins retreat to Corunna.

1809
January	Napoleon returns to Paris.
16 January	Moore dies of wounds at Corunna.
13 May	Napoleon enters Vienna.
27-28 July	Wellesley defeats French at Talavera in Spain, earning the title of Duke of Wellington, then retreats to Portugal.
29 July-30 September	British expedition to Walcheren in Holland proves unsuccessful.

1810
2 April	Napoleon marries Marie-Louise of Austria.
9 July	Napoleon annexes Holland.
27 September	Wellington defeats French at Bussaco, then retires behind Torres Vedras fortifications (11 October).
18 & 25 October	Fontainebleau Decrees: Napoleon orders the burning of all English goods found in France.

1811
5 February	Prince of Wales appointed Prince Regent.
March	Beginning of Luddite disturbance in England.
20 March	Marie-Louise bears Napoleon a son.
3-5 May	British victory at Fuentes De Onoro.
16 May	British again victorious, at Albuera.

1812
19 January	Wellington captures Ciudad Rodrigo.
February–March	Alliances formed between Prussia, Austria and France.
6 April	Badajoz stormed.
18 June	Britain and the United States of America go to war.
24 June	Napoleon's troops enter Russia.
22 July	Wellington defeats French at Salamanca.
12 August	British troops enter Madrid.
7 September	Indecisive Battle of Borodino.
14 September	Napoleon enters Moscow.
19 October	Napoleon begins retreat from Moscow.
5-18 December	Napoleon returns to Paris.

1813
February-March	Fourth Coalition begins to form.
3 March	Britain signs treaty with Sweden.
2 May	Napoleon defeats Prussia/Russian army at Lutzen.
21 June	Wellington wins Battle of Vitoria.
7 October	Wellington's peninsular army enters France.
16-19 October	Battle of Leipzig. Allies defeat Napoleon.
31 December	Prussian army enters France.

1814
	Allied armies close in on Napoleon.
31 March	Russian and Prussian forces enter Paris.
6 April	Napoleon abdicates.
11 April	Treaty of Fontainbleau.
3 May	Louis XVIII enters Paris.
	Napoleon lands at Elba.
1 November	Congress of Vienna begins.
24 December	Hostilities end between Britain and United States of America.

1815
1 March	Napoleon returns to France (beginning of the Hundred Days).
20 March	Louis XVIII flees as Napoleon enters Paris.
18 June	The Battle of Waterloo. Napoleon finally defeated.
22 June	Napoleon abdicates for second time.
7-8 July	Allies enter Paris: Louis XVIII returns.
August	Napoleon banished to St Helena (arrives 17 August).

INDEX

A Mariner of England 57
Abercromby, General 55
Aboukir Bay, Battle of 41
Acre, Siege of 53-4
Addington, Henry 4
Adventures in the Rifle Brigade 43
Alexander I, Tsar of Russia 16
Aliens Act 27
Allowance System 6
Amelia, Princess 15
Amiens, Peace of 4, 55, 60
Austen, Cassandra 22-3
Austen, Jane 11

Badjoz, Storming of 45
Bath 11, 23-4
Bellerephon, HMS 41
Bentham, Jeremy 34-5
Berlin Decrees 4
Betty, William "The Young Roscius" 11
Blake, William 35-8
boxing 11
Brighton 10, 13, 15, 18, 23
Brummell, "Beau" 10-11, 15-16, 17-21
Brussels 56
Burdett, Sir Francis 33
Burney, Fanny 22
Byron, Lord 11, 15

Camperdown, Battle of 41
Caroline of Brunswick 14, 18
Castlereagh, Lord 16
Charlotte, Princess 14
Chawton 24
Cobbett, William 12, 28-31
Combination Acts 27
Copenhagen, Battle of 41
Corresponding Societies 27, 33
Crockford's Club 11
Cuidad Rodrigo, Storming of 44-5

dandy 10, 11, 17
discipline, naval 58-9

Elba, Island of 5, 16, 46, 56
Emma 25
Evangelicals 12

Fitzherbert, Maria 13, 15
Fox, Charles James 14
Frederick of Prussia 16
French Revolution 26, 28

George III 10, 12-15, 52, 55

George IV, *see* Prince of Wales
Glorious First of June, Battle of the 41
Gustavus IV, King of Sweden 52, 56

Hazlitt, William 31
Holland, Henry 13
Hood, Lord 53
Horsfall, William 7

Income Tax 5-6, 11
India 51-2, 59
Industrial Revolution 9, 36

Jersey, Lady 14
Joseph Bonaparte 45

Keith, Admiral 55
Kemble, John Philip 11
Kew Gardens 28
Kincaid, Captain John 40, 43-7
Kleber, General 54

Lamb, Lady Caroline 12
Lamb, Charles 16
Lake, Lord 51
Liverpool, Lord 15, 28
Louis XVIII of France 57
Luddites, The 7-8, 15, 28, 31

Mansfield Park 24-5
Massena, General 43
McAdam, Robert 9
Methodism 12
Metternich, Prince 16
Mill, James 34
Mill, John Stuart 34
Moore, Sir John 39-40, 56
More, Hannah 12
Moscow, Retreat from 5

Napoleon I 3-7, 9, 14-16, 28, 30, 41, 46, 53-4
Nelson, Horatio 4-5, 40-41, 43
Ney, Marshall 44
Nore, Mutiny at the 27-8, 43, 60
Northanger Abbey 12, 23-5

Paris 57
Pavilion, Royal 14-15
Perceval, Spencer 15
Persuasion 25
Peter Porcupine's Gazette 29
Pitt, William, The Younger 5-6, 27, 30
Place, Francis 27, 32-5
Political Register, The 30-31
press gang 58-60

Prince of Wales (later Prince Regent, then George IV) 11, 13-16, 17-21

Repton, Humphrey 11
Richardson, Samuel 22
Richardson, William 43, 57-60
Rivoli, Battle of 3
Rutland, Duchess of 19

Sanditon 25
Scott, Sir Walter 25
Seditious Meetings Act 27
Sense and Sensibility 24
Seringapatam, Battle of 51
Settlement, Act of 13
Shipp, John 48-52
Siddons, Sarah 11
slavery, abolition of 12
Smith, Admiral Sir Sidney 41, 52-7
Songs of Experience 36-7
Songs of Innocence 36
Soult, Marshal 46
South Africa 50
Speenhamland 6
Spithead, Mutiny at 28, 42
stagecoach 8
St Helena 5
St Vincent, Battle of 41
Sweden 52

Terror, Reign of 29, 37
Tone, Wolfe 28
Torres Vedras 43
Toulon 53
Trafalgar, Battle of 4-5, 41-2
Turkey 52

United States of America, War with 4, 7, 9, 15

Victory, HMS 42
Vienna, Congress of 5, 16, 56
Vitoria, Battle of 45

Walcheren Expedition 43, 60
Waterloo, Battle of 5, 16, 40, 46-7, 56
Watsons, The 24
Wedgwood, Joseph 38
Wellington, The Duke of 3, 5, 16, 39-40, 43-5, 56
Wesley, John 12
White's Club 11
Wilberforce, William 12

York, The Duke of 39

HEATHFIELD SCHOOL

00003709